Writing Landscape

Taking Note, Making Notes

Linda Cracknell

IN THE MOMENT

Published by Saraband
3 Clairmont Gardens
Glasgow, G3 7LW
www.saraband.net

ISBN: 9781913393724

*Note: Units of measure are given either in Imperial or
Metric, depending on those best suited in each instance.*

Printed and bound in Great Britain by Clays Ltd,
Elcograf S.p.A.

1 2 3 4 5 6 7 8 9 10

Contents

Foreword

I went on my first walking holiday at twelve months old when my father put me on his back in the Alps. Walking and being outdoors – wherever I go – has been an important part of my life ever since. After moving to Scotland in 1990 I worked in education, and then for the World Wide Fund for Nature (WWF), gradually moving north and transforming into a writer by discovering the joys of both 'taking note' – small acts of attention – and 'making notes'. My fiction and non-fiction writing have become ever more linked to place, landscape and memory. As well as having travelled widely, I'm lucky to live now in the heartlands of Highland Perthshire, surrounded by hills, from where I've explored other parts of Scotland, as frequently reflected in these essays.

Map

Locations in this book

1 Ullapool
2 Inverness
3 Glencoe
4 Aberfeldy
5 Perth
6 Edinburgh
7 Glasgow
8 Exeter
9 Dawlish

Script and Scrape

I pedalled from the Highlands to the Lowlands over a small bridge crossing the Inchewan Burn. Squeezed into a valley formed millions of years ago when the Highland Boundary Faultline heaved south-west to north-east across Scotland, the burn separates, historically, two ways of life and a linguistic and cultural division between Gaelic and Scots. It was an August afternoon of intermittent sunshine and cool winds. The hum of the tourist-filled A9 harmonised with lawnmower and strimmer-buzz. Although linked to its sister village by Thomas Telford's seven-arch bridge over the Tay, a band of riverside woodland and Birnam's grey, high-gabled buildings keep Dunkeld and its famous cathedral hidden from here.

I parked my bike outside the arts centre – the Birnam Institute – and was immediately called into a series of conversations up and down the street with friends and acquaintances. This was cheery, vital chat about lives and words; there are writers and creative folk here, a superb second-hand bookshop and a community that cares deeply about the world and our place in it. Such reciprocal warmth was one of the pleasures of my afternoon's return.

Since 1995 I've lived only a half-hour bus ride or 90-minute cycle away, upstream on the Tay in a different valley. It was when I moved to Highland Perthshire that I began to write. Mighty trees, heather moorland and blunted peaks became my creative playground along with views that snake along sky-mirroring lochs, cascades and gorges reached by interlacing paths. In 2000 my first book of short stories was published and two years later I began to make my way as a freelancer – both as a writer and teacher of writing.

I stepped into teaching naturally, having always worked in an educational role. Encouraging others to write makes me curious about the practices of creative people and reflective about my own methods. I continue to be fascinated by *how* it happens, including the way our creativity sometimes gets on with the work subliminally while we focus elsewhere.

I've written the essays in this book over the last seven years. Some were in response to commissions, others 'commissioned' by the insistence of particular places or musings on the dialogue between landscape and creative processes. Many kept me close to home or took me to coasts and islands, into the elements, responding to tides and other natural rhythms, the cleverness of living things and excavations of human memory. I've found that immersion in a landscape will reliably spark up ideas and words. As a result, I sensed it might be stimulating and less inhibiting for new writers to be outside and in motion as they experiment.

The small weight of a notebook and pen in my pocket is my passport to feeling alive; I cannot help but be in the moment when translating observation and experience into words. We all have occasion to reach for words when a landscape rouses us, even for an Instagram post, journal entry, or a note to leave in a bothy book. But those less intent on writing *itself* can also gain from engaging viscerally and thoughtfully with the world and its sometimes-hidden wisdoms. The act of writing calls us to refresh our tired ways of noticing, and a writer perhaps has to look as patiently as a scientist, visual artist or naturalist does.

In the 1860s a period of ill health confined Charles Darwin for weeks in one room where he kept company with cucumber plants growing on a windowsill. In his enforced stillness, looking so carefully and long, he was the first to recognise the unique way in which a tendril of this climbing plant formed two opposing coils to attach and tighten itself to an inanimate support, demonstrating something like intelligence. Close observation of our living neighbours can be humbling. If we lie with our backs flat on the earth and look up through a deciduous tree canopy that will cast shadows there for far longer than the length of our own lives, or watch the collective sky-dance of starlings, we might adjust our acquired belief that humans are exceptional in the living world.

Darwin also knew that moving at walking pace is beneficial for thought processes, increasing our ability to make connections. He made deliberate circuits on a purpose-built 'thinking path' in his garden in order to develop his theories of evolution and sexual selection. Unsurprisingly, many fiction writers, both contemporary and past, identify walking as one of their necessary practices. I know that my own mind slips into an associative drift, thereby unlocking problems or plot points.

Despite the value of this mobile state of mind, to be properly attentive to what's around me I find I must pause, take out my notebook and engage with words. Sometimes I write 'HERE I AM' at the top of the page and note down all the senses, thoughts, feelings and things around me which define that state. After doing this I often feel lighter and freer in spirit. Attentive looking is frequently cited these days as a good thing in itself, honouring what is around us and elevated to a political act in resistance to the rushing momentum of inattentive change.

Once written about, places and living things tend to stay in my heart – I've made an investment and so an attachment. My allegiance to Birnam has grown because over the years I've led workshops here, delivered over a short but rich circuit of street, river-bank and graveyard. Most recently this has been as writer-in-residence for the Birnam Book Festival, but before that for several years each May I met a group of postgraduate geosciences students from the University of Edinburgh here. They came from all over the world, bringing to the woodland, paths and river their own filters of culture and language, character and inclination. These were writers of aca-demic theses rather than story or poetry, yet their tutors became convinced of the value to them of taking a train out of the city and being encouraged, over the course of a short walk, to pause for guided acts of observation, imagination and note-taking. It took them beyond dry research into immediacy and discovery.

When we reached the wooded riverbank I handed out blindfolds, one between two. They took it in turns to be a sensory guide to their blind-folded partner, the idea being to liberate the other four senses before the 'thug-sense', sight, strode in. There were damp knees, the scrape of bracken stems, noses pressed close to earth. An element of disorientation sharpens observation and for some participants, this experience surprised and thrilled them. Quite ordinary things became alien. The new birch leaf feeling like a slip of soft plastic. The rattle of dry seeds in broom pods evoking Brazilian maracas, perhaps with powers of divination.

The skin of faces and hands became more sensitive, responding to shade under that lovely canopy, then to sudden warmth on the sandy beach beyond it. One guide had their partner lie blindfolded with head hung over the riverbank for an intimate audience with the water-orchestra travelling east. Others tucked fingers into the great folds of an oak tree's bark and tapped to hear its hollow voice, or silked the trunk of a young birch. Admittedly facilitating taste was tricky (and potentially dangerous). One brave participant went so far as to lick the Birnam Oak as he spread his arms across its 7-metre girth. 'Lettuce', he announced, surprisingly. Connections were struck up between the woodland and inner selves, the scent of a grandmother's wardrobe remembered; time travel facilitated.

Sometimes I've felt as if the script is already there waiting to be found, that simply paying attention can tease words from the cracks in rock or allow me to hear them in a crow's cackle. And if there is to be a reader, words must convey sensation and place, coaxing our remote 'visitors' in amongst the trees to inhale the aniseedy scent of Sweet Cicely or hear the moistness of a blackbird's song. How else can writers communicate how it feels to be alive?

On each circuit of Birnam I collected words myself alongside students, and now my past notebooks surprise me as if passages were written by someone else. Over the years they bear witness to change. The arrival of beavers and their engineering of the riverbanks. The rise in spring of thickets of Japanese Knotweed like an army preparing to depart with lofted spears, and then their apparent eradication. The path that used to be straight until someone made a diversion around a fallen branch and everyone followed, etching a new way.

Once I'd reached the riverbank on the August afternoon of my return visit, I heard laughter and the babbling voices of summer visitors. Although it's an area of Scotland marketed as 'Big Tree Country', Birnam is famous for its literary connection to one tree in particular remaining from a forest with roots in Shakespeare's 'Scottish Play'. Three strange women who foretell the future, the eerie notion of a forest that might take to its feet, murderous ambition: all rich territory for the imagination. Perhaps it's not surprising given this background, that storytellers, writers, musicians and songsters have clustered here across the centuries and that visitors are still drawn in.

The 'Birnam Oak' is believed to have already been growing here in 1582 when Shakespeare was (perhaps) in a band of strolling players who put on a play in Perth. How could we *not* ask what it has witnessed in spanning the length of so many human lives, or what wisdoms it might divulge? According to the Woodland Trust, an oak tree is one of the greatest hosts of biodiversity in the world – supporting up to 2,300 species in exemplary hospitality.

Every visitor with a little agility, whatever their age, wants to crouch within the dark cave of the Birnam Oak's hollow trunk, or in the case of my students, see if it will accommodate all eleven of them at once. It seems to demand that we play like children. That day, above its carbuncled toe knuckles and the relief maps in its bark, I enjoyed its abundant leafiness. But since I was last here it had lost a significant limb, leaving a yellowed scar. I wondered who had taken the great branch away and what it might become.

We know the word *play* as an antonym to *work* and that by the 14th century it was in use for a drama, but its origins as a verb seem to have come from Old English *plegan* or *plegian* meaning, 'move lightly and quickly, occupy or busy oneself, amuse oneself; engage in active exercise; frolic; engage in children's play...'; all relevant to our sense-rich strolling. I've learned from language-lover David Crystal that in the writing of Macbeth, Shakespeare made great linguistic play by inventing numerous new words, particularly formulating verbs from nouns. Playing with word choices, as well as with our senses, is vital to good writing; and verbs drive text with concise power as well as offering myriad choices to add metaphorical nuance. Does the wind *batter* or *kiss* the oak leaves?

I enjoyed refreshing my ways on Birnam's paths that August afternoon. My imagination and compassion stirred at the graveyard of Little Dunkeld, where one stone told a story of William Ritchie and his wife Amelia Keay, who died a century ago and six years apart after having one son die on active service in 1918, another at the age of eleven months, and a daughter who died before she was three. It looks as though there was one survivor who lived until she was seventy-eight. I turned away from two much-admired nineteenth-century 'Adam and Eve' gravestones to walk back along the river towards tea at the Institute.

My steps kicked up memories of stories I'd witnessed students creating here. The truant child hiding from her pursuing teacher inside the Birnam Oak, who from her dark cave pelts the faces of any curious newcomers with acorns. A dog-walking undertaker with sheer soled shoes who has no content for a speech he has to deliver shortly at a Death Convention until he falls full-length into undergrowth and finds a new appreciation of leaf-litter and its promise, in death, of new life. And there's the woman who has just hit sixty, dyed her hair and found in the late-summer river a new slick partner that holds her close, caressing her skin. All prompted by walking this leafy riverbank in another person's 'shoes'. Nothing more than observation and imagination.

These are the essentials: the script and scrape of the landscape, allowing us to rediscover our own creatureliness within the thickets of the world, but also connect better with our humanity and find for it a voice.

The Great Affair:
Writing With the Flow

When I set off on a 21-hour journey from my home in Highland Perthshire in August 2019, I already felt in league with Robert Louis Stevenson. The Fellowship that was taking me to a village south of Paris was in his name, and I would stay in a house, formerly Hôtel Chevillon, which he had frequented in the 1870s alongside a bohemian crowd of artists from northern Europe and the US. It's now given over to creative lives and nurtures conviviality, offering potential once again for life-changing friendships. Winning the Fellowship felt affirming; permission to take time out of a busy freelance life to write.

But it wasn't just this 'permission' that excited me as I set off. 'The great affair is to move,' Stevenson had said, and a voyage was unfolding: Caledonian Sleeper, then the Eurostar. Trancelike, I was aware of an English summer passing beyond the train window: harvested hayfields, housing estates, a place called, intriguingly, 'Ebbsfleet', and the rumble of the line underneath me, the physical sways of the train. Closer at hand a fellow passenger told me a remarkable story of her American father's part in World War II France where she was going to celebrate the armistice with her triplet sisters. We were so engrossed in conversation we missed the murky dive under the sea and had to ask each other, 'are we in France now?'

I felt words being born out of motion; my observations sharpening with growing unfamiliarity. In the cloying city-heat at Gare du Nord the crowds evoked the clamour and bright cloth-prints of sub-Saharan African cities. Freed, later, from suburban trains and buses, I walked through the outskirts of the village in which I would stay, where a water tower rose like an inland lighthouse and road signs warning of leaping deer, pedestrians, horses, were strikingly distinct from those at home. Then into narrow streets of houses with chalky walls and large shutters. And later that chalkiness dissipating into an evening light that explained the area's magnetism for visual artists.

The intensifying effect on me of a journey to a new place was expected, more or less. It's when I feel most viscerally 'me' as a writer. And as I'd I said in my application, the nature of my writing – its focus on journey and a charting of my links to the sea and my seafaring ancestors – allied me to Stevenson. In August 1876 at the age of twenty-five he washed up here for the first time after journeying by canoe along the canals and rivers of Belgium and Northern France, which led to his first publication,

Inland Voyage. The journey generated something to write *about* and expressed his adventurous spirit, but perhaps he also made a statement by turning inland, having just turned his back on the family business constructing lighthouses and other feats of maritime engineering.

During his stays at Hôtel Chevillon he was protected from salt spray and granite cliff by 200 miles of land on one side, and a continent widening into remote distance on the other. Land-locked rather than sea-girt, his rebellion played out far from salt and family pressures, and with his liberated cousin Bob he found a bohemian 'family' amongst artists. Further summers here proved formative, and he changed the spelling of his middle name from Lewis to Louis. He also met Fanny Osbourne, resulting in a trans-Atlantic courtship and a marriage of adventurous travel which defined his short, often sick, life and the stories that he told, making an 'inkwell' of his ancestors and their seastorm legacy.

I was still to learn some of these details through literary osmosis from the house where I laid barefoot steps over his on the cool, black-and-white tiled floors. I liked to picture him slipping through the same high-ceilinged rooms 150 years earlier. He might sit on the terrace with a partial view through the heavy foliage of the horse-chestnut tree and down the small avenue of lime trees – not quite so dense and enormously tall then – watching light dappling on the river. And perhaps he'll go down the steps with Fanny or one or other of the artistic crowd who stay here, house-martins weaving flight paths over their heads. They'll feel the breeze more by the river, smell its slippery, celery-scent and watch skiffs come pointing through the arches of the bridge. 'If the evening be fine and warm, there is nothing better in life than to … lean over the parapet of the bridge, to watch the weeds and the quick fishes,' as he put it in 'Walking Tours'. They'll comment on the ducks, and the way the evening light casts an echo of each arch of the medieval bridge below itself, to form a perfect circle.

Books fell into my hands – Ian Bell's biography *Dreams of Exile*, Bella Bathurst's *Lighthouse Stevensons*. My allegiance with him grew as day by day, he became more alive to me. It was almost as if I understood him through the implication of what the place had meant to him, defined by the Loing river flowing weedily past.

I soon established daily rhythms. Motion, the 'great affair', was central. Setting the alarm for 7am, I'd leave the sleeping house after some yoga stretches to walk for an hour to orientate myself and improvise ways within the radius of my fixed point. I learnt the local landscape: gently undulating fields of stubble, unbroken broad-leafed forest where dry ground was scuffled up by wild boar, ex-gravel pits sailed by swans. The banks of the river called me but were often hard to reach because of private properties. But the canal which partnered it had a steady path and together the two watercourses became a focus as well as sometimes a barrier because of the few available bridges to allow a circuit.

As ever the rhythm of walking, the climbing sun burning off mist, warmed me towards writing, kicking up words, ideas, observations. I'd make a lively return to the small village, first calling into the boulangerie to buy a rustic loaf and usually a pastry, all carefully wrapped in paper, my clumsy French returning me kind smiles from the baker and his father. I'd carry strong coffee, cereal with yoghurt and fresh apricots out onto the terrace with one of the Stevenson books and my notebook to which each morning I'd add a new map of where I'd walked.

Seamlessly, as the sun's angle steepened, I picked up everything and moved down the garden, to sit under the trees at a small cast-iron saloon table close to the river. And now I'd free-write with no clear direction into an A4 pad for somewhere between 30 minutes to an hour. These pages together with the daily crayon sketches I set myself to do around the village – working in another medium but still exploring 'place' – built my confidence. I had paper-bound evidence of a creative output.

The human life of the river was waking up at this time, holidaymakers on the opposite bank assembling to swim, sunbathe, take to the water in inflatable kayaks, paddle-boards. Soon young men would be lining the parapets of the ten-arched bridge, taking it in turns to plummet with explosive splashes into the deepest part. None of this distracted me unduly, though it may have found its way into my writing. My daily exercises, my motion and flow, met and matched the flow of the river.

The next meander would take me back indoors, up to my first-floor apartment, my computer, the 'core work' that I had come to do outlining a new radio play; chipping out the pages of a book exploring family mariners, vagabonds themselves. From a dreamy, open-ended kind of state, I moved towards something more cerebral. *This* was the work, I kept telling myself, even though sometimes what I wrote closeted indoors at a desk felt dry, journalistic, lacking intuition as its drive. I also worried that I allowed too little time for it – the real work – amidst my walking and unfocussed creative routine. I grew anxious about progress and had to remind myself that walking, dreaming with book and pen and notebook and coffee, and exploring this generous location was also what I was here for.

Sometime into the usually-warm afternoon or evening, I'd head out to cycle lanes threading together river, forest, and similar villages; expanding my geography. Then on return a swim in the river avoiding the tangle of submarine weed but relishing the bright flash of kingfishers which sometimes swooped over my head. I raced fleets of ducks, eye to eye with them, and lost. And in the evenings there might be wine on the sultry terrace with artists and writers from Sweden and Finland, echoing the conviviality of Stevenson's time here.

On the outskirts of the village I'd stumbled upon the *Chemin de Stevenson*, leading out of the village across oregano-scented fields and tunnelling under the railway line into an extensive forest: 180 km (110 miles) of pathway I longed to follow. Then I'd have something to write about. Then I'd have the fluency. I wondered if Stevenson himself had experienced such conflict. The great affair may be to move but if you're a writer, you have to sit still long enough to make something of the experience.

Instead of taking to the long-distance pathway, the river's hold on me grew. I wandered down there at different times of day and at night when bats circled my head. My swims grew braver. Sometimes the weed gripped my fingers or waist and wasn't easy to shake off, but it bothered me less. The water was thick and green, deep with dark fishes. Swimming felt like dressing in water; wearing the river; un-sheathing from something else. Once I didn't shower after my swim and woke in the night to a feral pungency rising beneath the covers as if the river had accompanied me to bed or was oozing from my pores.

In the early mornings later in the month I looked upstream to where mist formed a discreet cover over the water. The river looked more secret, more tree-shaded there, disappearing around a bend. And I was intrigued by the name I'd seen marked beyond that bend on the town hall's map as *le bout du monde* (the end of the world). I tried to find it from the riverbank on a morning walk but it was frustratingly unreachable. I learned it was Stevenson who had named that place of shallows on a bend by a mill; he had gone there with the *Artistes du bout du monde* in boats. And hadn't they come to this village, departing from a colony at Barbizon, nearer Fontainebleau, mainly because of access to the river as well as perhaps the special chalky light?

Finally I hitched a lift upstream on an inflatable boat and then swam the kilometre back, a physical challenge not in my normal repertoire. My breathing became panicky at times but I had no choice but to keep going and I made my peace with the river, its silky green depths and hidden tangles, its quiet insistence on keeping going towards the bridge, the Seine and then towards the sea.

Even after only a week, but increasingly over the month, the central preoccupation of what I called my 'core work' began revealing itself in my free-writing by the river. It was unruly, unplanned, but 'felt'. And when I returned to the pages afterwards I found usable paragraphs, ideas, sentences. In addition to what had seemed the indulgences of observing locally or reflecting on creativity, I was now writing content.

A short story began to write itself in these hour-long shifts about a woman diverted from attending a conference in rural France, forced by an accident to spend days resting here alone, and taking to the river, divesting herself of something as if it was a skin or set of clothes. In the last week, notes about a new play began to flow over several days, animating the characters, their stories, so that I found I was writing in their voices. I was surprised by this – my 'core work' was now apparently getting done from my riverside seat under the shade of lime trees.

I began to realise that for the writerly mind, to sit beside a river is something like sitting on a moving train. A slightly blurred, only partly observed world passes. The river doesn't pause, there is constant movement and change only partially attended to, so that the mind floats, notes occasional details and forgets to resist the static nature of the desk. Flecks of light, foam, leaf, catch the light, pass, highlighting the water's speed by disappearing. The character of the river changes daily, even hourly, its colour darkening and velocity increasing after heavy rain, or with drought revealing more of the mud and stone bed it negotiates. And gradually comes an awareness of things plaiting beneath the surface: currents, darting fish, other unknowns as muscular as the trees that lean their trunks over it.

The great affair becomes the river itself, moving. The writer can sit still.

Lunar Cycling

My desk: a scatter of books, maps, letters, pebbles, and amongst them a relic which recalls me to another place, another daily pattern, another way of counting time. Mundane, yet treasured, this pedal from a child's bicycle is made of moulded creamy-white plastic and trimmed with two intact strips of reflector. I'll never know how it separated from its crank and chain and frame and wheels, or where it came from or whose foot once pressed it.

What's left of the spindle is rusty and encrusted with Acorn Barnacles. They also cluster on its surfaces, on one side sparse and tiny as punctuation marks; on the other, swarming in a small colony and anchored into crevices between the treads. I know now that they once swam in a throng of delicate *cyprid* larvae, until they dropped from the sea's surface with finite time to find a trustworthy home. Head down, appendages or leg-like 'cirri' up, they landed on the pedal and cemented themselves to it, growing six shell-plates around vulnerable head, gills and legs, whilst at the top four flat plates made a diamond-shaped 'door' to open and close with the tides.

This transformation, one of several including six stages beforehand as *nauplii* larvae, is as audacious as the butterfly's emergence from a cocoon, although in the opposite direction – from free-moving to sessile. For the remainder of their lives, which can be up to eight years, these crustaceans would remain fixed to a human tool of travel and revolutions; passenger-barnacles who cycled through the tides.

I found the pedal in the summer of 2017 during a month's stay at the Cove Park Artists' Residency on the Rosneath peninsula. Low-lying, with a higher spine of snarly moor and plantation forest, the peninsula dangles south into the Clyde with Loch Long to its west, bringing the wild to snag against the lawns of Victorian mansions at Cove. The waters of Gare Loch to the east bump up to caravans at Castle Point where holiday-makers from Glasgow swell the population each summer. Attached to Arrochar and its craggy 'Alps' only by a narrow isthmus, it was easy on this leg of land to imagine myself cut off. Once there, I designated as my fourth, northern, shore the road running coast to coast from Coulport, and committed myself to 'island' life.

I knew I'd need daily exercise, an escape from my desk, and that a new landscape would compel me to explore, so I decided to walk the entire coastline, tackling each section at the lowest point of the tide. Being there for twenty-eight days I'd witness a complete lunar cycle: two neap tides, when the difference between high and low water is smallest, and two spring tides around the full and new moon, when it is greatest.

With a tidal cycle taking roughly twelve and a half hours, I left my desk at a different time each day, gradually progressing from morning to evening. My days were regulated, but in a way, irregular; my low-tide walks an unbreakable daily appointment offering a cosmic discipline and a stroll with a sense of purpose. 'Ardpeaton for the 9.52', I recorded in my notebook on day eleven, as if I was catching a bus. The next day, I caught the 10.41.

Using my bicycle (pedals still attached), I circled the twelve-mile loop of road to a different coastal point each day, finding rocky shores, occasional mudflats, little bays of sand and shingle, leggy jetties. In this way, I learnt the place through its shoreline, with its pillboxes, fishermen, mussel beds.

Where deciduous woodland met the coast around Rosneath Bay, the canopy had been salt-pruned by spring tides so that during the ebb, foliage hung to a sharp horizontal line well above the shore. High tides had also quarried soil away leaving tree roots cage-like, proud of the bank, reminiscent of mangroves. Occasionally I passed CCTV cameras, signs for Neighbourhood Watch, and experienced a shiver of surveillance. Walking around Rosneath Point one evening beside uneasy, clattery woodlands I passed a fire which had been left raging and unsupervised on a boulder whilst curlews and oystercatchers called and seals howled from Perch Rock.

Although the range between high and low-tide is moderate here, a significant space opened up when the sea withdrew. My explorations developed a pattern. I first crossed the wet 'intertidal zone' to reach the water's edge, sometimes over rock slippery with bladder-wrack. Watching for waterborne birds or vessels, I'd feel the wind direction, notice how a change in weather often accompanied the pendulum swing of the tide. Then I'd step along the wet space, teeming with visible and invisible lives following their interwoven biologies. Tidal pools captured a marine microcosm of fixed creatures or slow-movers, encrustations, vivid colours, the dance of light and water, things that waft: a lavish chest spilling treasure that had nothing to do with me.

I also observed the strandline where the spring tides leave their gifts. It's not uncommon for gunshot cartridges from Newfoundland to be washed up on Scotland's west coast as well as 'drift seeds' from tropical waters, in folk custom marvellous enough to hang as a charm around a neck and be called 'puzzle-fruit', or to find soil and grow into something exotic.

On each walk I took photos, made sound recordings, scribbled about sensory observations. Alongside rafts of eider on Loch Long, I noted a flotilla of warships and tugs escorting a nuclear submarine out into deep water. It must have been one of the four Vanguard-class submarines based at Faslane on Gare Loch, skirting Rosneath to load Trident warheads at Royal Naval Armaments Depot (RNAD) Coulport, before setting off on a lengthy submerged patrol somewhere in the world.

At twice the length of a jumbo jet, the submarine riding the surface of Loch Long with its long vapour trail and fanfare-flotilla seemed both furtive and highly visible. Once I'd witnessed it, the peninsula between these two colonised Clyde lochs felt snarled in a Cold War past which has rallied peaceful protesters since the 1960s. Improbable developments, when you consider that Coulport was a holiday destination for Glasgow gentry and former home of the nineteenth century Kibble Palace glasshouse now erected in Glasgow's Botanic Gardens.

A police boat always lurked offshore as I wandered, its angled bow suggesting targeted binoculars. Inevitably one day it brought a friendly police officer in a car to enquire why I was walking towards the sentried razor-wire fence defending RNAD Coulport – razor wire which, as I pointed out, would be totally ineffective at low tide when I could simply walk around it.

Without having planned to, I began to gather a few objects on each walk. Initially I homed in on those that pleased aesthetically: pebbles or pearly-lined shells, tea-cup or mug handles, coloured glass scoured to a dull beauty, and chinks of blue and white china once so cheap it was used as ship ballast. Perhaps these were beachcombing clichés. Although I also photographed a dead rock-goby, a jellyfish with its rosette of minute red compass gradations, rocks draped with Trump-like hair, I mostly collected human-made things: train tickets, a doll's head, fishing floats, a blue plastic fisherman's glove separated for ever from its (g)love-lorn partner.

Different stretches of the coast offered different human debris. Apart from the ubiquitous tampon applicators and bottle lids, there was less plastic on the inland reaches of Loch Long than on the eastern shore close to the caravan park, where Helensburgh glittered across the water. Domestic ceramics from garden pots to porcelain lay in fragments close to the villages. Red bricks from Accrington. Tiles were the currency on Portkil Point near the village of Kilcreggan along with the wrecks of 'leadless glazed' toilet bowls from Shanks and Co Ltd in Barrhead, a company world-renowned in the nineteenth and early twentieth centuries for innovations in plumbing and sanitation. But it was entanglements of the natural with the manufactured which increasingly became my collecting focus.

We seem to have no adequate common word for the place uncovered at low tide: the 'littoral' is slippery in our understanding. A place that isn't always there, reeking of repellent odours. Ungainly on two legs, we don't seem to belong, whereas wading birds, molluscs, crustaceans and specialised plants know how to live there. Yet this place of continuous renewal is an important source of food in many human cultures. Edible shellfish gathered here were once known in Orkney as 'ebb meat'.

When the shore is sandy, gradually sloping so that the waters retreat a great distance, most lifeforms are buried under the sand and it appears barren. It invites us to walk out onto a shiny no-man's-land that lays another sky beneath our feet. Here we might fall through into a different world, or a seal might adopt a human form. This space between two identifiable states has fostered a long-standing belief that no one can own it.

Our contemporary human lives march in circadian rhythms, according to dark and light, the twelve-hour, twenty-four-hour clock. Perhaps tidal rhythms seem irrelevant unless we are bait-diggers, shellfish-pickers or seafarers dependent on certain states of sea to leave or return to a port. Or perhaps we believe we can outsmart cosmic forces.

In coastal communities it used to be thought that death could only come during the ebb. Survive the turn to flood and all was well, at least for the next twelve hours or so. Tides bring us the solace of reliable change. During my Rosneath stay I'd often find myself cycling breathlessly on one of the upper lanes at the time of high-tide, exhilarated by Arran's serrated skyline and the red-and-white-liveried ferries plying between Gourock and Dunoon. High tide seemed to trigger high energy, whereas intuitively I found the ebb melancholic; a time for wandering and pondering.

Tide times are predictable; the tables published long in advance. That our ancestors found them orderly is summed up by our word 'tidy', indicating 'things as they should be'. And the intertidal zone itself is characterised by everything being in its place; disciplined bands for different kinds of life, all observing the tides in their own rhythms. Barnacle settlements point to the limit of the 'upper shore' as defined biologically, leaving anything higher up to lichens and periwinkles, the most tolerant to drying out.

In Scotland we never live more than sixty or so miles from the coast, yet find tides mysterious. As humans we are 60 per cent water, our female reproduction cycles relate in some half-remembered way to lunar ones, and even our behaviour is understood by medical experts to be affected by the full moon.

Sensitised to these cycles myself during that month, I noticed poor sleep a few days either side of the full moon, felt an onrush of creative energy as the new moon began to swell. I've long been obsessed by weather forecasts when travelling to different parts of the country, but since then, if the place is coastal, I've also established the state of moon and tide. The flicker of a buried pulse in me makes me wonder: despite the decline of the moon's magnetism, might we still harbour responses to lunar and tidal cycles in our bodies as periwinkles apparently do even when removed to a lab?

Peaton Layo is a curved spit of land stretching from a shallow stony beach into Loch Long. From my cabin I dropped steeply on a hawthorn-hedged path to cross the Coulport Road, wading through a field of meadow flowers to arrive at a changed flora breaking through shingle – clumps of white Sea Campion – known in Gaelic as the 'little sea cauldron' for the shape of its sepal tube, fleshy stonecrop, sea plantain, sea asters.

From the spit, a small bay scooped away either side of me, each ringed with parallel lines of deep-red seaweed archiving the various heights of the tide. It was here on day sixteen, midway between a neap and spring tide, that I found the barnacled bicycle pedal cast up high and dry. It seized me with its visual quip on the contrary pulls of settling and travelling, although in maintaining a roaming life, perhaps these cycling-barnacles made a bad choice. But it also spoke of nature's way of using what we discard, how our relics might be colonised once the Anthropocene is over.

I'd noticed barnacles coating every solid surface around the shoreline. They scraped my hands as I scrambled on exposed south-westerly-facing rocks, where their cone shape keeps them resilient to surf-lashings. They have long been regarded as a nuisance for 'fouling' the sleek hulls of boats and thus slowing them, or clogging up engine intakes or exhausts. They may be chiselled off. An industry has been made out of poisons to stop them settling. Yet the infamous power of the barnacles' lifetime cement means another industry has emulated its qualities for glue manufacture.

Their colonies spread a distinctive patina on rocks which, imagined on a different scale suggest antique lands, each volcano uniquely patterned with converging ridges and gullies. Close up, they resemble a field of old men's tobacco-stained molars. So abundant, so immovable, so still, we may think of them as stone.

But a wet, barnacle-gnarly rock stopped me one evening as I wandered an emptied-out Culwatty Bay. Reflected sunlight pulsed all over its surface. Under a magnifying glass I saw through the film of water the shells' diamond-shaped hatches opening and closing, their hair-delicate 'legs' wafting together in a net to catch plankton. The sight thrilled me. This was a privileged insight into a small, pulsing life previously invisible. Rather than inanimate, the barnacles came alive in my mind and were, literally, kicking. If and when the rock dried out, the shells would close, trapping aerated water around their gills, allowing the creatures to sit out a period of even considerable heat until the tide turned. Hard-wired into them are rhythms of immersion and drying out; their feeding and breathing is deter-mined by the gravitational pull of sun and moon, revolutions of the moon around earth and the alignment of both with the sun.

Semibalanus balanoides, these most widespread of barnacles, depend on a low mean sea temperature for breeding. With warming seas now, I wonder if they will move northwards as part of the current mass relocation of species. Marine life is said to be moving four times faster than the land-based. Estimates vary, but Britain's coastline, fractured by unique collaborations of tide and geology, is as much as 20,000 miles long with the main islands included. I picture the barnacles industriously trac-ing every rocky inlet and craggy peninsula, encir-cling us within a fortified wall. It's a familiar and disregarded feature of our salted sometimes-shores. My month of observing tidal patterns, treading places defined by the reciprocity of land and sea, taught me to treasure it. And my relic-paperweight helps me to remember.

Getting Away From it All?

There's nothing like boarding a ship for a sense of liberty. When I wheeled my bicycle onto the CalMac ferry heading across the Minch to North Uist, my panniers were packed with camping things, sketchbooks, pens and colour pencils. As ropes were cast from the quay, I felt I had slipped my responsibilities.

In the summer of 2016 I signed up with the University of the Highlands and Islands for a one-week summer school, 'Art and Archaeology', based at the arts centre, Taigh Chearsabhagh. North Uist is one of those entrancing Hebridean islands with curving shell-sand beaches and particularly rich heritage of Neolithic chambered cairns. Spending three days with an archaeologist in the field and two days responding creatively seemed sure to bring relief from the clamour of words and the frustrations of the novel I was 'parking' back home. I was intent on forgetting my narrative (which was about forgetting) for a while. Perhaps I would reach back into the visual world of my fine art education in the early 1980s instead.

I've always been drawn to remnants of lives embedded in ancient landscapes: the stones of Avebury, the Uffington White Horse. The layering of mysteries often surfaces in my writing and is explicit in my novel *Call of the Undertow,* where cartographers delve into mythic as well as material remains. But I also think of the *process* of fiction-writing as archaeological.

I learnt on North Uist that the making of a stone circle might have been more meaningful than the resulting monument; how to scrape at a midden to reveal strata of bones and burning; the use of a 5 x 5 grid to make an accurate site drawing. I learnt about the palimpsest, buildings on top of buildings, revealed, for example, by excavations on the northwest peninsula of Udal which proved a continuous legacy of occupation from Neolithic times through to the nineteenth century.

It was on these successive layers that archaeologist Iain Crawford was to concentrate for thirty years, from the early 1960s onwards. His discoveries included circular buildings from the Iron Age peculiar to this island and now thought to have been homes but referred to as 'wheel-houses'. Extraordinarily, the knowledge that he gained wasn't published at the time and therefore wasn't shared. Additionally, the location, far out on an Atlantic promontory, means that remains are gradually being eroded by storms. Here was a story of erosion, tides, encroaching sea and amnesia.

Amongst the finds were two quartz pebbles painted with curved lines and dots. They're similar to decorated pebbles found in Caithness, Orkney and, particularly, Shetland. Experimental archaeology suggests that the long-surviving pigment was made from distilled peat tar, possibly connecting them to metal workers. The origin and progeny of the Udal stones are not yet determined, but the Shetland equivalents are dated from the middle through to late Iron Age and into the Pictish period. It's speculated they were charms of some sort.

I decided on this place, and these pebbles, as the focus for my creative work, and cycled to Udal, pitching my tent on the Western dunes. For the next twenty hours I had a two-mile long, west-facing beach to myself. At low tide I collected twenty-five washed up quartz pebbles – the whitest and smoothest ones. I let them dry for a short time and then painted designs onto each with waterproof inks. I used a wide palette, but imitated the original patterns – Saltire-like arrangements of curved lines and dots, and other simple motifs. I loved the materiality of the whole experience: the clack of the stones together, the ink and sand on my fingers.

My writing process often involves physicality. I understand the interaction of characters with specific landscapes through explorations on foot. I sometimes sketch as a way of getting under the skin of a place – a way of making my narrative real and material.

Getting Away From it All?

On my Atlantic beach, engrossed by observing the sun and tide as my process gathered its own momentum and rules, problems with my novel could not have been further from my thoughts. I raced the high tide to prepare my pebbles, ran up and down the dunes to my tent, took photos, documented time and stages in my notebook. At 6.32 pm I committed words in black waterproof ink to the reverse side of the stones. Each of the twenty-five had some significance to the place I was in and the story of encroaching amnesia.

The tide reached its full height at 7.15pm. Wind came up and the sky suddenly cleared, the low sun highlighting white sand, the weathered grain of a timber post, my rows of stones waiting, luminous. Extensive views opened north to the peaks of Harris and east across the grasses and flowers of the machair to the island of Oronsay. Finally the retreating water allowed me to settle my 5 x 5 pebble grid. It was a game with the next high tide. Afterwards, I'd discover which words the sea had selected for my 'found poem'.

By 9.25 the next morning the sea had been in and out far enough to reveal its choices. But on the still-wet sands, it was clear that, unlike the pigments I'd mimicked, my so-called 'waterproof' inks had not stood the test of this blink of time. I wandered the shoreline, found quartz pebbles whose shapes seemed familiar, but were blank. That is, all except for two. Both had lost their coloured pattern. But one remained clearly marked with the word 'wheel' and another retained a ghostly remnant of the word 'share'. Appropriate words, I felt. The wheel of time. The need to share memory if it's not to be eroded.

I cycled back to Lochmaddy to rejoin my fellow students. I'd forgotten from my art college days the conviviality of the shared studio, where ideas transfer – sometimes wordlessly – and spark against each other. Some of my peers had taken an oblique, playful approach to past, present and materiality, mimicking archaeological processes and producing artefacts like I'd seen in the work of Cornelia Parker. Emulating archaeological methods, I collected my two lightly-marked pebbles into small bags, categorised and recorded them as 'findings', and constructed a small book in which they appear. My outcome was negligible, yet I felt content.

I learnt about archaeology as a discipline that week too: the territorialism arising from individuals 'belonging' to a particular institution, defining themselves by period, approach and geography. How they might refrain from using imagination as a method of understanding the past, even though in our own discussions we agreed that our experience of being human could itself provide insight. And I learnt of the tendency, and danger to a community's learning, of some archaeologists continuing to *dig* rather than writing up and sharing their knowledge.

When I returned home to my novel, I quickly realised what should have been obvious to me, that my protagonist had trained as an archaeologist and was aware of the possible dangers of being a 'digger' rather than a sharer. The erosion of memory was central to both stories, at home and away. It turned out that this 'time out' was an opportunity for my subconscious to find a different way of looking at my material while I thought I was off-duty.

The Painting and the Verb

'You've never heard of Joan Eardley?'

His startled look unsettled me but my eye continued to follow a white lane until it converged with a tumbling row of single-storey cottages on the skyline. Hanging above this strange land, a full moon smudged a gunmetal sky. Somehow it was obvious the sea lay out of sight below the village. A yellow sea fog filled my lungs. I was alone on the lane when all other human life had shrunk indoors.

Why had I never heard of an artist who could so viscerally move me in a landscape?

I admitted to my ignorance. 'No, I haven't. And where's Catterline?'

It was 2006 and I was in the art room at Langholm Academy, where the single member of the department, David Proudfoot, was gazing at me in astonishment and then encouraging me towards more of Eardley's work. I was there as part of an experimental programme – Arts Across the Curriculum – running for three years in a number of Scottish local authorities, in which writers and artists worked alongside teachers, helping to find a creative way into mainstream subject matter in primary and secondary classrooms. It was a great education for me through topics including energy, geology, 'India', caring and decision-making in the community, soundwaves (in Physics), democracy (in Modern Studies). The art class was of course by nature already creative, but the challenge facing David was getting his students to *write* personal responses to paintings as the curriculum required. Students in three S1 classes (twelve to thirteen years old) had to write how a painting made them feel, what it made them think of; some kind of response. Anything. Could I help?

David's art room was in an eyrie at the top of the building; self-contained and culturally apart from the Academy-ishness of the rest. I saw the way the pupils, a few of whom I'd known in their final year in local primary schools, responded to his casual manner, to a space in which they could to some extent be themselves, where music might play in the background. Whilst some rules were relaxed, others such as taking creativity seriously and respecting equipment had to be observed. The room held a certain magic for at least some of the pupils whose individuality seemed to be recognised.

David had reproduced ten paintings by artists including Ann Redpath, Steven Campbell, Picasso, Monet and Turner. Two of Joan Eardley's were included – one of Glasgow Street children and this one I was staring at from Catterline with its confident but somehow sketchy realisation of a winter village. He said the pupils were usually flummoxed about what to write and how to structure it. I gave them some questions – 'What would you smell, taste, hear if you were inside the painting? What does it remind you of or make you think of? What's about to happen?' – and so on. I modelled a response: 'The Moon leads me along the snowy lane and I can smell peat smoke from the cottage chimneys. My hand is slippery on the snowball I carry. This painting makes me shiver.'

In particular I encouraged the youngsters to register their reaction with the most active part of speech, emphasising the careful choice of the verb, the 'engine' in a sentence, for its power, delivery of nuance, means of being concise. So much can be quickly understood about a man who slithers into a room as opposed to one who stomps, or the difference in atmosphere when a tree bristles under moonlight rather than glistens. I gave them lists of verbs to try out if they were stuck, to describe elements of the painting but most importantly to convey its effect on them. Does the painting yell at you, whisper, sing, or does it *tell* you something? What does it make you want to do – jump, vomit or laugh? Writing took us into the territory of both thought and feeling and soon their initial observations quite naturally began to transform into imaginative pieces of poetry or prose.

David and I were both delighted by the writing produced. As one of the ten paintings was Peter Howson's *Just Another Bloody Saturday* (1987), it wasn't surprising that many of the boys chose to write about football:

> 'I smell the players' sweat
> While I'm eating my chips
> I hear the crowd cheer
> While I'm eating my chips...'

Several chose to write about Eardley's *Street Kids* (1949), speaking for one of the children pictured: 'I stole an apple from someone's garden and we all had to run because they might see us. There were sparks like fireworks from my tackety boots. We found a newspaper and Elizabeth read to us. Peter caught his breath while I ate my apple and listened.'

For evaluation purposes at the end of the project, we asked the pupils to complete the line: 'Writing about paintings for me was _____'. They added words like 'cool', 'strange', 'eye-opening', 'really embarrassing', 'exciting'. They completed, 'When I go to an art exhibition for real, I'll look at paintings _____' with: 'as if I'm nosy', 'carefully, for a long time', 'as if they tell stories'. I still think about those wide-eyed first-years who must now be adults and hope that some of them have realised these intentions.

Although few chose to write about *Catterline in Winter*, the painting still insisted on leading my eye down that snowy lane and sent me on a much wider journey into Eardley's landscape work. In 2016 I went to the Scottish National Gallery of Modern Art exhibition 'A Sense of Place' and was struck once again by the immediacy of her preparatory sketches and paintings. At Catterline I lay inside a summer field with its corn ears and flowers captured in the paint itself. A flurry of overlaid pastel put me amidst the scratch and scent of a rich autumn hedgerow. Energetic bursts of line and shade stood me in the face of an approaching storm.

Learning about her dedication to working out-doors, the articulacy of her body as well as mind in creating her work was a powerful confirmation to me of my own treading of paths and exposure to grazing rock or mountain height as part of my own creative process. Her story seemed to validate my thrill in finding words and stories by being in the elements and often alone.

When asked about her artistic influences, she said: 'As a matter of fact my greatest influence is looking at nature. I never look at other paintings at all.' The excitement I felt at her work also reinforced my impulse to *look* as a way of knowing, showing me that literature and fine art are not so far apart after all. The line or brushstroke, like the verb, vibrating with life itself.

The Writer, the Island and the Inspiration

Not everyone enjoys the experience of being alone on an island. Forced to eat limpets, buckies and periwinkles, some of which made him sick, young David Balfour, used to being landlocked in the Lowlands, never did make peace with his 'horrid solitude' when he was shipwrecked on the Isle of Erraid. It rained continuously for nearly three days and he had only 'dead rocks, and fowls, and the rain, and the cold sea' to talk to. Ignorant about tides and assuming himself surrounded by sea, he hailed passing boats as he circled his prison, but was ignored and left hungry.

I wasn't knowingly a fan of Robert Louis Stevenson (RLS), but once I was living in Scotland, from 1990, and referred to as a 'Scottish writer' since 2000, his work became part of my adopted literary inheritance. The meaning he took from travel, particularly journeys on foot, chimed with me. Some of his *Treasure Island* characters populated the Admiral Benbow Inn, a familiar landmark when I visited my mother in Penzance, and I glimpsed his family's lighthouses in my travels around Scotland on headlands and far skerries. They have long illuminated my imagination as elemental monuments with potential as dramatic crucibles.

But it wasn't until 2019 that I picked up *Kidnapped*, for many years unread on my bookshelf. Perhaps I was partially drawn by the cover of the Penguin Popular Classic which shows a detail from 'Voyage to the Pacific' in which a square-rigged sailing ship is cresting a wave in a churning sea just off a high, rocky headland. So I began to read.

Here is a lowland boy, orphaned, betrayed by an uncle, shipwrecked on the West Coast and forced to walk across the war-torn and rugged landscapes of Scotland as he becomes a man. He travels with a diametrically opposed Highland character. Lost, disorientated, an innocent, he is unprepared for the physical challenge, but learns about life and his country as he goes. The author's passion for people and human nature surfaces as visibly as the sea and landscape in all its harsh romance. So I was surprised to learn that RLS wrote it in physical confinement resulting from the ill health which had often kept him isolated in his bedroom as a child. The novel came close to remaining unfinished.

Before travelling to France in summer 2019, and having now read *Kidnapped*, I made a mini-pilgrimage to the Isle of Mull's western peninsula, the 'Ross of Mull'. And then, to where, at its far western tip, Erraid is connected and separated by the tidal pulse.

The Writer, the Island and the Inspiration

I'm intrigued by tidal islands; a threshold open-ing and closing in a rhythm cosmically determined. I wanted to arrive there under my own power – bicycle and then foot – and then be contained, surrounded for another twelve hours, forced to appreciate nature's disinterest in my needs. I was intrigued by the idea that a space that was land when I set out on my jour-ney would transform to sea. A drawbridge raised.

As a voluntary castaway rather than an enforced one, my experience was as different as it could be to Balfour's. June sunshine sang over me as I pedalled, with my load of camping gear, the 40 miles from the ferry landing at Craignure, over a high pass towards the tip of the peninsula. I finally stopped on one side of an inlet tapering from the Sound of Iona towards the place where the two land masses of Erraid and the Ross of Mull come closest to touching.

I'd timed my arrival for low tide at 6pm. But far from being dry, a small estuarine river ran midway, and it was clearly deep enough to prevent me taking any chances. Only later I understood that as this was the 'neap' period of the tides, when the moon is midway between phases of old and new and has least magnetic influence, the difference between high and low water is smallest. In contrast to the tidal conditions for David Balfour at full moon, for me not only was high water not so very high, but neither was low water so low.

A farmer directed me to a place further around the coast where I'd be able to cross. Abandoning my bicycle, I struggled across fields carrying bike panniers loaded with enough food and 2 litres of water to allow me to stay a single night. I stepped across a narrow stretch of white sand and barely lengthened my stride over 'the sea' between islands.

Cheered by landfall, I climbed from shore to plateau and dropped my bags. Flickering bog cotton marked soggy channels ahead but there were no obvious paths, no visible 'Balfour Bay' on an island only a mile in diameter. Abandoning one of my panniers, I set off with the other, following a compass bearing I hoped would lead me to it.

I sweated across the highest ground, ankles scratched by heather and bog myrtle. The scrape of barren terrain went on until, without warning, the scale suddenly flipped, and the sea appeared below me. Between me and it was a narrow green valley leading to a slot of white sand which widened between a pair of granite cliffs striding south-west, out into the sea. Even from a distance it was clearly the paradise I'd imagined. The bog relented and my steps quickened as I dropped down, small hills rising around me, till I was on sheep-cropped, firm turf above the sand. A cobalt sea waited beyond. There was no yacht moored in the bay, no other tent. I had the place to myself.

Within an hour I'd returned for the other pannier and the tent was up on the grassy bank. I was alone with rock-pipits, plovers, sandpipers whistling the place alive on a long, cool Midsummer night. I walked barefoot down the shallow burn which carved the sand with feathery branches resembling the bronchioles of lungs. At the beach-proper, the bite of seawater on my toes told me I would not swim. But I paddled in a lagoon which crossed the beach, trapping a mix of salt and freshwater against a rise in the sand. It was brackish and warm.

When planning the trip, the short length of my stay seemed determined by the unavailability of fresh water. But now I found that, although unmarked on my map, a small burn ran towards my camping spot just before driving through turf to drop to the sand. There were sheep here so its cleanliness was not guaranteed, but I reasoned that by boiling it for five minutes, I would make it safe.

Because of the effort of getting here, I immediately decided to stay not one night, but two. The weather promised well for the next day and I wanted to sink into the place. My adventure in cycling from Craignure had already purged my restlessness.

Balfour's 'horrid solitude' was now possible. But that first night on Erraid I relished being alone, and an escape from what I had witnessed earlier at Fionnphort, the ferry port for the Isle of Iona.

While consuming takeaway langoustines and tea, I'd watched a boy of about eight in round spectacles bagpiping ashore strangely quiet tourists from the ferry as they returned to rows of coaches. The procession seemed to go on and on. This shock of mass tourism in what we think of as a remote place, was later compounded by the sight of a cruise ship, luminous in low sunlight, looming like a tower-block first over the tiny island of Staffa and then the harbour at Iona.

I was unhurried, free to enjoy simplicity. To sleep, stroll, boil water for tea, munch oatcakes and cheese, stare at the lengthening shadows and the strike of last sun on white sand. Not for the first time I wondered whether I've been designed to be a desert-island castaway, to live unobserved amidst the small patrols of sheep and the cormorant family out beyond the shore. One flew in and out from a nest deep in the cracked granite, delivering the catch. Their cackles were amplified by rock, conjuring monstrous creatures. Barnacles clustering on seaward rocks charted the sea's departure and return in their breathing and feeding, their shell doors opening and closing with the tides. I heard birds pipe on from within my tent until at least 11.30pm. The night temperature plummeted and I slept in thermals with the sleeping bag hood caught tight over my head.

The Writer, the Island and the Inspiration

I relished my own 'exile', reconnecting with my seventeen-year-old self on her first cycle tour with a tent. No one, including my parents, knew exactly where I was. I met people, solved my own problems and fended off harassment long before the days of mobile phones. It was a thrill, that first independent adventure. I inhabited my true self, or another version of it. I also discovered that I was more gregarious than I knew, but that the comfort of talking with another person could sometimes be traded for dialogue between pen and notebook. Such travels, I believe, gradually led me towards a writing life, with travel in it. When taken alone, such journeys offer keen exposure to adventure, adversity and joy.

Stevenson was far more expert on the sea's ways than his character, Balfour. He said of his family, the 'Lighthouse Stevensons': 'whenever I smell salt water, I know that I'm not far from one of the works of my ancestors'. There was pride, and a lifelong maritime-affinity. In a letter to Henry James written from Honolulu in 1889, he wrote, 'though the sea is a deceitful place, I like to be there ... and to draw near to a new island, I cannot say how much I like'.

This dissonance between the writer's knowledge and his Balfour character's ignorance drives the novel's sea-drama. Tricked aboard the square-rigged brig, 'Covenant', at South Queensferry, Balfour is dizzied by the sheer scale of the ship, the unfamiliar humming of the tide and sailors singing as they haul ropes. He's carried off as a prisoner towards slavery in the Carolinas. Sea-shaken through the Northern Isles, the ship's Atlantic crossing is thwarted by adverse winds and they are forced through the Minch, south to the Inner Hebrides.

They're still underway when Balfour notes the moon, nearly full. Whilst he couldn't have known the effect, his creator does, commanding lunar magnetism to accentuate high and low water in a spring tide. Not content with that, he 'moves' the infamous Torran Rocks 20 miles or so closer to the Ross of Mull. Add a captain without a chart and the ship is now in a sea 'thick' with rocks.

Kidnapped is set in the mid-18th-century before the famous Dubh Artach lighthouse was built. The need for it in this major shipping channel had been well made by countless losses on the lengthy archipelago of rocks which RLS wrote of elsewhere as 'an egg-shaped mass of black trap, rising 30 feet above high-water mark. The full Atlantic swell beats upon it without hindrance, and the tides sweep around it like a mill race.'

As the ship begins to struggle, Balfour observes how the brig is thrown about by the tide and three strong men struggle with the tiller. Just as a reef is spotted to windward, the sails empty. On the rocks, the brig falls onto her beam and he into the sea, 'hurled along, and beaten upon and choked, and then swallowed whole'. However, once the tide race has flung him out, he's able to struggle onto the south-west shore of the island of Erraid, at Tràigh Gheal, a place usually now spoken of as 'Balfour Bay'.

Cold, wet and weary, he spends the night walking to and fro along the 'desert-like' sand with a sense of terrifying aloneness. From higher ground at daybreak he sees that he's imprisoned by the sea on a small island and so his manic circling begins.

When Balfour finally understood the word 'tide' shouted across the water by a fisherman, and realised that at the ebb he could simply walk onto the Ross of Mull, he berated himself for not understanding better the ways of the sea. Admittedly he was unlucky on his three or four days (and it was convenient fictionally) that each time his circular prowl of the island brought him to the gut between Erraid and the Ross, he found it flooded by the high tide rather than fully emptied.

The words *inland* and *island* are visually so close; a trick, a slip of one letter away from each other. It suggests a congruence. On an island one is surrounded by water, a 'castaway', whereas inland we might feel swamped by land. As David Balfour found, one may induce a longing for the other.

Perhaps I understand his compulsive looping better from today's perspective, writing in the time of Covid-19, which has kept me treading within a more or less domestic radius for months. Lives seem both mundane and extraordinary. Lashed by the language of the sea, statistics are characterised as 'surges' and 'waves'. The numbers of dead are announced daily, and sometimes I imagine the terror of being isolated in hospital with lungs mechanically pulsed in ebb and flow.

I realise that, at first, confinement released me into acute appreciation of a glorious spring. I explored more thoroughly than I have in twenty-five years of living in rural Perthshire, discovering new paths, ruined villages, listing bird species spotted and rediscovering the names of flowers. A particular delight arose from the ritual of climbing to a west-facing rock on a small hill, sometimes carrying breakfast and a flask of tea, or with a bottle of beer in the evening. Gaining a sense of perspective, I could watch squalls approaching from the hills beyond Ben Lawers and look down on where I live – the compact grey stone town encompassed by moor, forest, field – where a safety net of relationships is woven. I knew that I was fortunate.

Nevertheless, over the months, my landlocked location began to tumble me into dreams of past travels, voyages, shorelines and horizons. On my inland-island I sometimes felt the loss of touch-stones in the literary world, the wider world. But I felt most disorientated by the coast – usually a mere 60 miles away on either side of me – decamping beyond reach. Sixty miles became a forbidden distance, vast and dangerous. Above all in these months, I have longed for the sea.

Being forcibly stilled for wider travel made me realise how much my wanderlust and restlessness usually determine my life. The previous year between March and August I'd walked limestone Alps in Austria, taught residential workshops in the English Dales and in the Cairngorms, visited my mother in Cornwall, and spent Easter in Sussex. The whole month of August was spent in France at Hôtel Chevillon.

RLS had spent time on Erraid when his engineer father was quarrying and building the lighthouses at Skerryvore and Dubh Artach. It must have had a powerful effect on him at nineteen because he used it as a setting three times, not just in *Kidnapped*, but also in the story *The Merry Men* and in an essay reflecting on his time there, *Memoirs of An Islet*, in which he said: 'I steeped myself in open air and past ages'. Not in the engineering calculations his father might have hoped for.

Before choosing the life of a vagabond and writer aged eighteen, he travelled Scotland with his father on the annual lighthouse inspection, and later served his apprenticeship with the family business over summer vacations from civil engineering studies at the University of Edinburgh. Unimpressed by some of the coast, he called Anstruther 'a grey, grim sea-bitten hole'; Wick 'one of the meanest of man's towns, and situate certainly on the baldest of God's bays'. But other aspects thrilled him. While in Wick he took a trip in a diving suit to watch underwater builders, felt the ground under him 'quail' in a storm, and witnessed the North Sea's power to destroy the harbour developments not once, but twice (to the Stevensons' professional embarrassment).

In his essay 'The Education of an Engineer' he summarised the incidental delights of the profession: 'It takes a man into the open air; it keeps him hanging about harbour sides, which is the richest sort of idling; it carries him to wild islands, it gives him a taste of the genial dangers of the sea...'. But he scorned the desk-work that followed, shut in an office, to draw or measure or wrangle with figures.

Caring 'for nothing but literature' he took 'a memory full of ships, and seas, and perilous headlands, and the shining pharos', and crafted fiction from them. Ships sail through his work; tide and storm generate drama between humans and nature. Stories of the sea's isolating power were passed down to him. Whilst building Dubh Artach, thirteen men and the resident engineer were besieged for two weeks by an Atlantic storm, captured in their barracks – an iron pod on legs teetering on a rock. Erraid, used as the shore station, was 15 miles away from the reef and unreachable. RLS learnt how a storm at sea might capsize men's minds or how fellowship might arise from shared terror.

After a short stint as a lawyer, having rejected the lighthouse business, he cast himself off from family to become a writer.

Morning sun penetrated the yellow inner tent at 6.30am with surprising heat. I heard bleating and looked out. Grey-white wool on grey-white sand; they were barely visible. It was only the contrast of one black sheep that tutored my eye on the subtler shades of the others, settling cold-night bones on warm sand. Knowing that this was the hour of the morning's low tide, I walked to the beach barefoot on dew-jewelled grass and then icy sand.

Turquoise in retreat, the sea was poised to rise up the beach again. Newly exposed granite on the shore was marked by a few feet of plimsoll-line black lichen. And a small new bay was reachable by rounding a corner. It was a more secret place, skirted by pillars and blocks of granite and giving way to grassy banks rising towards the great western arm that reached into the Atlantic. Beyond it, I could see the isolated rocks and skerries on which Balfour's ship and many other non-fictional ones came to grief. But for now I had no need to explore further than my beach, the grassy ledge where I camped, and the burn that travelled through it.

I returned to sit outside the tent as growing heat burnt off the dew, boiled water and felt the keen rush of coffee. A light aircraft droned somewhere, and the odd pleasure-boat passed. Two luminous kayaks slunk silent lengths into the next-door bay. It wasn't even 9am and yet the world was already alert to the peculiar beauty of this day.

I became aware that a golden eagle wheeled above me, reinventing its shape by leaning its head or bunching its shoulders or braking with parted wing-tip feathers. It came and went over the course of the day, sometimes so close that its brute grace caught my breath. When the eagle was absent a gang of ravens took the air above the cliff. Boy-racers cavorting with the thermals, their boisterous croaks and shrieks were reserved for the most echoey places.

Even when horizontal in my tent with no view, the place pulsed on conspicuously.

The rhythm of walk and pause, day and night, activity and stillness over several days – just as RLS describes in 'Walking Tours' – is my usual urge. On towards the new. But here I was content to settle, paying respect to a particular place and easing myself into its ways rather than imposing mine. Tide. Breath. Day and night. Waves washing a little closer or retreating.

I left the bay for a while that afternoon when a pleasure boat came in and emptied a family onto the beach. It wasn't unexpected, but in any case I wanted to get up higher and to see the observatory on the north-west corner of the island, which I knew had served as a communication system with the lighthouses during their construction. From that vantage point, as well as the entire eastern coast of Iona, the rocky, western shore of Erraid was revealed. I could see a yacht below sheltering amongst the skerries from increasing north-easterly winds. 'Pippin', I read through my binoculars.

I lingered at the restored circular observatory, enjoying inside the way its two windows and door framed the panorama into horizontal slices of sky, sea, land. I read the story of the lighthouse building, learning that fifty souls had stayed on the island during the quarrying and construction. And then I wandered down to see their cottages on the north-western shore and the quay, all still solid and robust as one would expect of a Stevenson legacy. The project brought granite-working experts from Aberdeen together with Gaelic-speaking hammer-men on the drills. It must have been an interesting cultural meeting. In 1872 they were affected by a scarlet fever outbreak on the Ross of Mull, and then by an epidemic of rodents on the island.

I pictured a young RLS striding out and loitering just as I was, with his writerly sensibility raiding caves and crags and bogs for fictional opportunities. What kind of character would be tricked by the inconstant tides? Perhaps he was already imagining a dramatic episode for a young man, an inlander and Lowlander, alone here, stranded and hungry, wet-through from his wrangles with the sea and missing his companions. Such an imagination must already have been distancing him from his father, making him dreamy and aloof. 'I shall be a nomad, more or less, until my days be done,' he wrote to his mother in 1874, emphasising the restlessness he had always felt, perhaps invisibly to her. He told her how he would watch the trains leaving Edinburgh and long to go with them.

As I returned across the highest point of the island, I could see that in Balfour Bay no further tents had been erected and no boats were anchored. I walked on in bliss.

Whilst following the burn towards my tent, I saw a turquoise garment abandoned on the bank. Going to pick it up, a movement in the deep cleft where the burn dropped to the beach startled me, and I glimpsed the back of a human head. Copious grey hair straggled to shoulder length. I continued to my tent, wondering why someone would be hiding here; at least that was what it looked like.

Distracting myself with books, notebook, binoculars, I noticed after a few minutes that the garment had gone. Perhaps the person had climbed out and walked away up the valley while I wasn't looking. But I found it hard to relax into the coming evening without being sure I was alone. And that piratical wild grey hair: I pictured some vagabond unhinged by sea or solitude. Would the head turn to face me with an eye patch or gruesome scar or long red beard?

After a few minutes a smiling woman approached me along the sand. Almost apologetic. Long grey hair. She'd come ashore from a boat to wash in fresh water, knowing this small burn from previous visits. She joined me on the grassy ledge and in that half-hour sitting side-by-side, looking west, we talked only of meaningful things. She was travelling with her husband on the yacht I'd seen from the observatory. They moved slowly up and down the ragged coastline from their island home. The day before, she'd waded through puffins on Treshnish. We found common ground quickly. She always came ashore, she said, in order to explore on foot, while her husband liked to stay with the boat. They had found a formula for adventure despite the rheumatoid arthritis which has hobbled her longer walking adventures.

She was a beautiful woman, tanned from days at sea, hair tousled and her story luminous. We had no need to build barriers in such a place and whilst we were alive on that grass ledge flecked with grains of white sand. As we talked the arms of granite framed gradations of blue from pale near to us to the deep ultramarine of deeper, wider seas. The wind rose. Ravens squabbled above us. And I relished this human company in my castaway state.

I am not an island. I want to be connected, to be a piece of John Donne's continent, just as this 'island' of Erraid is connected intermittently to its mainland. Perhaps, along with many other writers, I have contradictory impulses. The desire for both reflection and activity, stillness and travel, solitude and connection. And the way our lives are pulled between poles play out in each case differently. I can enjoy both being landlocked as RLS was in Northern France, and sea-girt. But here our tidal island imposes connection to another shore, and at other times, isolation.

Then Helen walked away from me across the sand in her wellies and long coat and was folded into the rising green to the west; moving back toward her boat 'Pippin'. And I folded back into my solitude. At what I took to be low tide, I walked the shore-line once again. The Paps of Jura peaked on the horizon, and closer by, dark blue shadows lay under cliffs. Birdsong lofted in whirlpools above me.

Periwinkle and 'Chinaman's Hat' shells had been washed up on the long, low-tide shore and I followed lines of fragmented algae, which each incoming wave had deposited. In some places, looked at from shore to sea, the inland line was solid and precisely laid, and above it, like a strip of hieroglyphics lay a scattered geometry of algal shapes in diverse colours; a mysterious script which I didn't know whether to read from left to right or the reverse. An archive of the tide.

Looking inland, low light shocked white sand flat but pronounced the granite above into high-resolution wrinkles. A deep blue sky above.

Twenty-four hours after putting up my tent, I lay down in it again, still wide awake but content to listen. I knew that the cormorant swooped in and out of a shadowy notch to deliver fish, the Golden Eagle soared across the roof of my world, and the plovers piped and ran along the ground in sudden starts. They didn't need me attending to them.

My own days at Hôtel Chevillon were hot and summery. But one day early on, it was overcast and in the relative quiet, fleets of ducks took their opportunity to reclaim the river. Fish rose with silky slops. I watched a large, dark bird fly downstream. It wasn't one of the herons I'd seen before, but I didn't recognise this bird until it rose up from beneath the river's surface close to the bridge and twitched its head repeatedly; a large and beaky head. Then it eel-dived, oily and slick and I knew it as a cormorant.

In his flush of liberation, with the comfort of surrounding land unfastening him from family and Scottish sea squalls, how would RLS have reacted when a cormorant surfaced, stowing under its sleek feathers a reminder of brine and tide? Would his thoughts be recalled to a gaggle of dark birds on some tide-torn western skerry – ragged characters drying their wings in Atlantic wind? That hint of salt water might thrust him before disapproving ancestors. Would he feel unable to escape his legacy as an only child who disappointed his father and family, bringing to mind his defence in the poem *Underwoods* of 1887:

> Say not of me that weakly I declined
> The labours of my sires, and fled the sea,
> The towers we founded and the lamps we lit,
> To play at home with paper like a child.

His popularity arose first from stories of adventure drawing on the sea and ships – *Treasure Island* in 1883, written as a serial for children, and then *Kidnapped* in 1886. His eventual success required audacity, persistence, even when no one wished to publish his work amidst general confusion about who he was writing for. For much of the twentieth century, following his death in 1894, he was known principally as a writer for children.

Yet it's his travel writing and his essays that I particularly enjoy. He captures the freedom of being on the road alone and taking life as it comes. The throwing off of usual restraints, the casual encounters, and the dialogues that arise between solitude and company, the road and the stopping places. Days and nights under the stars, the body and the mind in motion. The pure joy of independent journeys.

It was perhaps why, when Fanny returned to the USA in 1878, and he considered himself 'the miserable widower', he took comfort from walking with a donkey in the Cevennes. Justifying this journey, he wrote: 'I travel not to go anywhere, but to go; I travel for travel's sake. The great affair is to move...' and the sentiment of the often-omitted extra phrase: '*And to write about it afterwards*': a recognition that writers need experience as subject matter.

I'm always confident that the mesh of body and mind in walking motion will drum up locations and characters for fiction or provide insights into life, or even into myself. Travelling alone might be thought of as isolating, yet it can intensify meetings with others along the way. RLS wrote, about finding company at the end of a day, that it is 'as if a hot walk purged you, more than of anything else, of all narrowness and pride, and left curiosity to play its part freely, as in a child or a man of science.'

In 1879 he jumped aboard a ship from Greenock to New York in pursuit of marriage to Fanny Osbourne. She was ten years his senior and still married with children, so their relationship was hardly likely to meet with approval from his family. His sudden departure in secret from them may not just have been about rescuing the relationship. Could it be, as Ian Bell suggests in his biography, *Dreams of Exile*, that it was also a necessary adventure in order to have something to write about?

His onward journey of thirteen days to Monterey, California, saw him haunted by the interminable plains beyond the train window and the difficult lives of his fellow passengers, but also by his own appalling psychological and physical state which after arrival laid him low with pleurisy, malaria and serious haemorrhages. The extreme he was pushed to became material for his writing. Perhaps some of us who focus on place and travel and adventure in our writing observe more closely and imagine more deeply when we enforce our own creative exile – whether on a new continent or by separating ourselves from those who care about us. Or, perhaps, by arranging to be encircled by incoming sea on a tidal island. We make a laboratory of ourselves.

His life was defined by a drive for freedom, in which he seems to have hurled himself from exile to exile, seeking experience and a climatic cure for his lungs. On his second Atlantic crossing, when he and Fanny left for the USA from Bournemouth – her domestic bliss and his domestic prison – he relished the storms on the seventeen-day voyage. Finding a fresh opportunity to reinvent himself and his work, he wrote to his cousin Bob that he had, 'forgotten what happiness was'.

I was reluctant to break Erraid's spell the next morning, but nagging at me was the question of leaving. My food had stretched to a second unplanned night, but I had only four oatcakes remaining, a serving of couscous, some cheese. The longer I delayed, the later in the day I would have to cycle off into what was now a strong north-easterly, a headwind.

I explored the arm of embracing granite to the west, returning to pack my sleeping bag and mat into their respective bags. Then I sat within the shelter of the tent door. I seemed to be waiting. But for what?

Having seen no one all day, I was surprised by a figure walking slowly towards me across the sand, a big stick in hand, binoculars, a hat disguising the face. We both waved as she approached and materialised into Helen, strolling towards me from the good ship Pippin.

'You should have come to the shore and waved,' she said when I explained my dilemma about staying. 'We've got a ten-week supply of food on board. What do you want?'

And I thought of David Balfour and all his frantic waving and shouting which brought him no help at all, making memories of his time on the island still horrible, even at the end of his cross-Scotland adventure. And here was I, desperate to stay and enjoy my huge privilege, finding assistance easily.

A little later I walked back across the island with Helen through deep bracken, crossing rocky inlets inlaid with shells and weed only ever washed by spring tides. When we reached steep rocks tumbling into deep water, her husband James rowed the tender across from their anchorage. While I waited they rowed back to the boat and returned with a tin of mackerel, shortbread, oatcakes, a carton of grapefruit juice and a good helping of muesli for the morning.

The sea was irritable, pulling at the little boat as they passed over my supplies. Having exchanged addresses and promised to keep in touch, we each let go and they scudded back towards Pippin while I returned slowly to my tent, secure now for another night, feeling that there was nothing else at all that I needed.

Because it was cool and the ravens seemed to give me permission with their own antics, I played on the beach, climbing a vertical black set of steps up a two-foot-wide faultline in the granite. I listened to the wash of the waves retreating and coming in, the brief silence in-between like the bottom of a breath before the next inhale. And I tried to synchronise with it. I found the sea's breathing took only a little longer than mine.

I've wondered whether people who live in intimacy with the sea find in their lungs an echo of tides or the rhythm of waves? After the outbreath, the depletion, a brief stillness like a stretch of rock or white sand emptied of water. Or a slack tide before the flood rises. The empty point emulates death itself; a blink of doubt as to whether life will return. And yet in it comes: the flood in of water to the bay, oxygen to the lung. The renewal of life itself.

But the lungs of Robert Louis Stevenson were treacherous and marshy with pleurisy and consumption, his tidal rhythms far from certain. Breath came in gasps and sputters. I discovered in this an etymological irony. The word 'lung' derives from High German *lungun*, literally meaning the 'light organ'. Its original meaning is only now remembered in the English idiom to, 'punch someone's lights out'. 'Light organ' seems to flicker with the spirit of his family's 'sea-lights', a mission bringing greater safety to so many seafarers. However, the word 'light' here refers to their tiny weight, rather than luminosity. Nevertheless, the breathing of life into characters, stories, landscapes by the rebel RLS is what the family is best remembered for now. His 'inspiration'.

Having spent time in France at a place where he was perhaps most active and in his best health, I'm especially aware of the ill health which dogged his life and abbreviated it at forty-four years. It seems remarkable that it was so defined by travel and adventure considering his appalling physical condition for much of it. But ironically his illness, as well as his writing, seems to have driven the travel itself, towards the best climate for his lungs. When he and the family set off from San Francisco in 1888 for the South Seas on the yacht Casco, the 'great affair' had resumed. He shed another skin. But this time he never returned.

As low tide approached, I made a sketch of each new type of washed-up seaweed and I looked them up in my seashore book, as much because the names are evocative as from any need to know: grasswrack, bladderwrack, sea lettuce, dabberlocks, and then one which was like a sheet of pasta with frilly edges. According to the book this was *Laminaria saccharina,* or seabelt or sugar kelp. Or, it may also be known as 'poor man's weather glass'. With that, my grandmother hobbled onto the stage of my imagination, tapping her barometer ritually once-a-day.

She clearly didn't entirely trust it because she also consulted the piece of seaweed that hung in her small cabin at the back of the house, a custom that came with her from Braunton to Exeter via her sea-captain father who died when she was only seven. I suppose her seaweed was this 'poor man's weather glass'.

Before retiring to my tent, I ran up and down the beach to fire up my circulation and warm my numb feet. The tent zip had been broken by the wind. I woke at 2am with the sound of water closer. The high tide. The energetic time. I lay listening to it and reading. I didn't mind being awake, luxuriating in the long light of June in the North and happy to feel myself once again confined by an encircling sea.

I heard the first bird at 3.30 am. The sheep began complaining at five. At some point in between, I heard a snipe quivering its strange, sonorous chorus, drumming across the little theatre in which I seemed to be living.

It was too windy for the stove to work safely in the morning. This time I didn't hesitate but packed up swiftly and completely, realising how willingly I would have lived on like this given time and supplies; prolonging my intimate exchange with the place. I sensed that staying still in such a location for longer, a human would inevitably become more elemental.

An experiment for another time.

I stopped briefly at Fionnphort and ate an egg roll, millionaire's shortbread and a peach in quick succession, with two mugs of coffee. Back in the world of tourist buses and money transactions, tables and chairs, I must have looked a wild woman, flushed with the outdoors, hair stiff with salt and sand, eating ravenously and spilling crumbs and coffee on the floor. The spell was beginning to be closed. I had stepped out of the circle, the amphitheatre in which my world had turned for three nights with birds, tides, sheep.

I pedalled off into a battering wind as I knew I would have to, towards the evening ferry from Craignure, pushed and jostled and occasionally almost halted by the sometimes northerly, sometimes easterly, sometimes in-between wind. Halfway along the Ross of Mull, I reached a high point overlooking the up-combed surface of Loch Scridain. It was one of those beautiful moments of synchronicity. Against the monumental buttress of Mull's great wilderness, the Ardmeanach peninsula – which concludes dramatically at its west end in a 1000-foot cliff – was a classic sailing ship. She was sailing powerfully despite scant canvas – two jibs and a staysail, and a much reduced, reefed-down mainsail. I was on the leeside so she leaned towards me, driven by the thrust of wind and sea from the north-east, and throwing up a thick white bow-wave. A single figure was visible at the wheel. A brave course set out of the shelter of land.

It was exhilarating to watch, and I felt what many of us probably do at such a sight. It's hard to define exactly, but I know that it causes even a sea-hardened fisherman to reach for his camera. As well as the visual spectacle, the conjuring of Stevenson and his pirates or brigands, it throws a line to our own history and the elemental nature of our ways upon this planet.

Many of us gasp at the vision of such a ship without needing to understand what's involved on board. But I was thrilled that day by a visceral sense of this 115-foot-long vessel; the spray and speed, strain of canvas and creak of rope and timber. Even at a distance the sight through binoculars brought alive in my body the memory of turning the Bishop Rock Lighthouse off the Isles of Scilly a year before.

Four miles off the nearest inhabited island, at the furthest western point of Great Britain, the lighthouse tower drew us towards it, our hands rough on hemp rope, trimming as a team those same foresails so that they and the wind cooperated as one great curved blade. We were in some of the most treacherous waters of these isles, the pale tower growing in height to its full 49 meters as we approached, sea hissing, readying to go about.

The construction of this lighthouse had been another extraordinary engineering challenge, though not a Stevenson one. Built to mark a small rock ledge and taking the full force of the Atlantic Ocean, the first attempt was destroyed by the sea. It was completed in 1858 after seven years of labour during which men were carried to and fro by small boat from a cottage on a nearby islet, as tide and storm allowed.

Joy swelled in me with this small miracle, this wrinkle in time and geography, as I realised that without doubt, I was watching the Braunton ship, Bessie Ellen, first owned by the family of my great-great-grandmother, Emma Chichester. And here she was, still magnificent over a century after her building, far from her Cornish home port. I waved and waved and waved. And I laughed out loud, breathing in excited gulps.

For sure, I had steeped myself in open air and in past ages during my stay on Erraid, and here was the physical emblem of both appealing to me in my slightly deranged and sea-salted state. My true self, or a version of it, released from island-exile and throwing a line out again to the wider world.

In Solitude Where
We Are Least Alone*

As I descended from Am Mam, sunlight was being
ushered out of Camasunary Bay and the green valley
which leads away from it by the leaning shadow of
Skye's soaring Cuillin. I was relieved to have in my
sights the old cottage, which made a bothy there,
after being buffeted and whipped all day by an
autumn-equinox gale and with nearly two weeks of
walking an old droving route already behind me.

As I approached the bothy, I saw through the
bay window a tranquil interior and a table on which
lay a book and pen. It looked like a writer's desk
that had been left especially for me. No-one else
was inside and I was glad of that, realising that my
tent would not survive the winds and I must sleep
indoors. I've never experienced the famous cama-
raderie of an impromptu 'bothy night' but I didn't
think I wanted one just then. I wanted to reflect,
revisit my experience, write in my notebook.

Thinking myself sheltered at last from the wind,
I fetched water and while it boiled, explored the
bothy. There were four small rooms, each with hard
sleeping-benches, and a large 'sitting room' with an

---

* From Lord Byron's 1812 narrative poem 'Childe Harold's Pilgrimage'.

ash-filled hearth and a clothes-dryer dangling from the ceiling, but no firewood. Once a home, this building now shelters the fleeting souls of walkers, climbers, overnight partiers. They had left traces of themselves in a squalid muddle of abandoned things – bird skulls, empty beer bottles, a packet of Sweetex, a collection of hard-hats, a brass candle-holder, a sock, a bible, a copy of *Private Eye*.

I returned to the 'writer's desk' and watched the light die on the sea.

The place descended into darkness. After a lull the wind growled towards the cottage from the shore. I held my breath before it hurled itself in a full-frontal attack, battering the cottage front. It sounded as though the waves themselves were lashing at the windows; buckets of water sluiced them. Masonry creaked as anything loose on the outside of the building was tugged at and torn. The storm continued in a sustained onslaught, rain following wind in volleys of steel-tipped darts. Reluctantly, slowly, it relented briefly, leaving windows rattling. A singing wind-tune filled the gap between squalls, high-pitched as a cartoon ghost. Then came the aftermath – water spurting, streaming downwards off the building through pipes and gutters.

Mice chewed on through the performance with teeth that sounded like tusks. A clock kept ticking. I made hot chocolate.

Perhaps bothies are one of the few places where as a matter of course people will write with a pen about a walk or a place in a 'bothy book'. In this way, words get left as well as detritus. I felt bound to read from the book at Camasunary. Interspersed with simple stories of sunshine, rain, otter sightings and the pursuit of mountain tops, were bizarre entries suggesting half-demented sex-starved men. I was glad no-one else had come.

Two entries though, caught at my imagination, and made me close the book. In March, a German visitor had written: 'Something terrible life there. I'm scared. I can't explain but in the night it screams like a dog-sheep mutant murder fish or something. It's horrible.' And in May, anonymously: 'Did not believe in ghosts or supernatural before I stayed here overnight. I do now! Never want to experience that again. Glad to be gone!'

The wind continued to rattle and shake at every ill-fitting window. It sought entry points, sneaking to the back of the cottage when the front resisted. I had no candles and no spare battery for my head-torch. In any case, the torchlight only made giants of the shadows that lay beyond. There were too many places creaking and groaning with secrets. I crept away to my chosen bedroom at the back of the cottage and shut the door.

'Aren't you afraid?' was the question I was most

frequently asked by people I met on my four-teen-day solo walk to Skye from Perthshire. I didn't understand what they meant. I have always felt safe in a tent and I was mostly camping well away from people. Or did they mean the fear of injury or being lost? I didn't want to be left dying in the hills, that much was true. But when I thought about the journey before I set out, the anxieties were mostly about the possibility of loneliness, the emotion of returning to places, the ignominy of defeat. Not fear exactly.

I had wanted to spend this night alone but my imagination, sparked by a few written words, was intent on making solitude a hell. The drovers, I couldn't help thinking, would have been good company for each other in such a situation. I wished that someone else had been there.

I lay in my sleeping bag, denying my own inter-pretations of sounds beyond the door. Breaths and gurgles startled me but turned out to come from my own body, strangely amplified. I held my breath in anticipation of the heavy latch pulling back on the outside door to signal late arrivals, other kinds of arrival, imagined a pause while they stalked the cobwebby rooms. I tried to prepare myself for my bedroom door opening without warning, and not being able to see in the dark or in torch-glare who had opened it.

I felt pressure growing on my bladder but ignored it, unable to walk through those dark rooms full of other people's residues and the scuttling of things in corners, to the safety of the outdoor rage. I waited, adrift in a storm-lashed ship with my thoughts and impressions. I thought I heard the latch crack open at one point, then nothing. My conscious and unconscious minds wrangled with each other, conjuring sensations and dreams. I heard a Landrover arrive and was aware of the building filling with young soldiers. They played loud music and I had to ask them to turn it down.

When I woke to light seeping through the salt-smudged window, the gale was still roaring, but between the laden clouds were stretches of blue. No-one else was there.

The place was calmer for me in daylight. It had given me a psychological ordeal but like the affection you might feel for a wild horse or dog you have tamed, it made it seem my own. Intermittent squalls flattened the rushes and blew sea-spray against the bothy despite the low tide. I saw occasional flashes of light along the coast at Elgol – car windscreens and doors catching sunlight as people arrived in the harbour to see the most spectacular view in Britain, and to be told there would be no sailings of the *Bella Jane* today.

I knew I couldn't, or wouldn't, spend another night at Camasunary but I wanted to stretch the day, enjoy the place alone before walkers from Elgol, Kilmarie, Sligachan, even Coruisk, staked their own claim on the bothy and the beach. Despite being alone there, the night had felt busy, crawling with image and thought, marauding dreams. Around mid-morning I saw a man pass the bothy window fighting the wind for his jacket. He didn't come in but hurtled onwards.

I stayed for the whole morning, taking a chair outside between showers, watching oyster-catchers bob along the shore, a gull flying shells up from the beach and then dropping them to float down again and retrieve its smashed prize. The air outside felt warmer, the wind softer. Waves rolled onto a beach lined with seaweed. I took disproportionate pleasure from filtering coffee into a mug, walked the shingle as I drank it.

Then I looked inland along the valley that follows the dividing line between Red and Black Cuillin. Gently rounded on the east, fiercely craggy on the west, built from granite and gabbro respectively. I felt my journey drawing to its conclusion after an evening with the gods and a night of paralysis. It was as if I was waiting for the return of the 'ordinary world', the inevitable acceptance of the end to the line I had walked across Scotland,

and the turning for home. This wrangling with my crowded solitude had been a necessary and dramatic finale.

I packed my rucksack, and turned north to the valley that would walk me towards tea, cake, company, the end of my journey: the famous Inn at Sligachan. And what would have been the starting point, the gathering point, for the drovers, their cattle and their dogs before they headed south.

How to Be Free

Amongst the fraternity of walking writers, I fall into step with Robert Louis Stevenson who opens his essay 'Walking Tours' by dismantling the idea of their purpose as principally to *see* landscape. Instead, he highlights the sweet dialogue between the 'march' and the evening's rest, the rhythmic chain created during a walk taken over several days. Coming to rest is for him an active element to be appreciated, savoured all the more for the walking itself being relatively short. For Stevenson, the 'overwalker' misses out on the very happiness sought, evoking the proverb of the person who 'goes further and fares worse'.

Although I sometimes choose to walk a long, footsore day in the Scottish hills, or take a week or fortnight on the trail of former walkers, in the last couple of years my habit, especially when time is tight, has become to walk somewhere special for just one night with a tent and food on my back. Using my body to reach a place where I lie down in direct contact with the earth and then turning back towards my everyday life sings of simplicity and purpose. To move, expose myself drunkenly to fresh air and the elements, and to step into a rhythm which offers a particular kind of creative thinking frees me from responsibilities and brings a sense of well-being. It becomes a pilgrimage of sorts in which I both lose and find myself. A good walk offers an opportunity for transformation.

So it was that in late May I found myself on one of Scotland's greatest short walks in Glen Coe, a walk that my fellow-mountain-lover and I had last taken, separately, in the 1980s. Perhaps I had not returned for the very reason of its lure and convenience, reached as it is from a place where the roadside car park commonly teems with people disgorged with cameras from tour buses. Rocky pillars and buttresses tower on each side of the narrow glen, which twists seaward with its burden of white water and snaking vehicles. Glen Coe's drama is highlighted by a tiny number of human settlements amidst the austere architecture wrought by volcano, ice and water. There are lofted birds, mountaineers wrinkled into high crevices, and the place remains haunted by the story of a massacre.

The 'Lost Valley', little more than an hour's walk from the car park, was once secret enough for the cattle belonging to (or stolen by) the local MacDonald clan to be hidden there. It's also said to be where some of the fleeing clan took refuge on the wintry night of February 13, 1692, while their neighbours were killed. The entrance cleft is invisible from below, concealed behind a steep wall of rock reached by a climb to 300 metres. The valley has become less 'lost' or secret since the National Trust for Scotland built a footbridge over the gorge of the Coe and signposted tourists towards it. Its popularity can be gauged by the polished stone underfoot, burnished like kitchen quarry tiles by family groups or mountaineers. In all seasons those seeking the most expansive views skirt between the triple spurs branching from Bidean Nam Bian before climbing to the summit, at 1150 metres the highest peak in Argyll.

We set off in sticky heat uncharacteristic of a Highland evening and followed the path and its narrow steps through welcome shade. Slant light cast the towering buttresses of the Three Sisters into slate-blue shadow whilst illuminating spangled birch leaves below them. Up we went through twisted silvery trunks and tangles of lush foliage, patches of bluebell and violet scattered alongside the steeply-falling burn. Behind us, when we turned, the V-shaped cleft, tangled with spring leaf, framed a segment of the main road and above it the wall of weathered rock on the north side of the Glen. There, other skyline climbs were revealed. Am Bodach, the 'old man', stood as the eastern outrider of the famous Aonach Eagach ridge, which convulses towards the coast, partnered just to the east in a separate massif, by the wrinkled face of A' Chailleach, the 'old woman'.

Sweating under our packs loaded with necessities (and non-necessities such as cool bottles of beer) we longed to dip in the deep pools that we passed but pressed on up the steep gorge until emerging into a boulder field that spread narrowly around us. We sensed the threshold of our quest, and soon after came the heightened moment of any pilgrimage when the destination is glimpsed. Despite all our foreknowledge, it remained a revelation.

Lying a little below us a perfectly flat and expansive valley floor opened, scattered with shingle and at this near end, with boulders the size of houses – the largest single rockfall feature in the whole of Great Britain. On three sides rose sheer mountain walls, building a high, undulating ridge above. The most accessible point for mountaineers was distant but directly ahead of us, its penultimate steps still covered with large patches of shadowed snow.

If you look up the Lost Valley on Trip Advisor, it is this moment of surprise that many people comment on, the large ice-flattened valley suddenly coming into view and earning the name and the enigma. We shared it as equals with the many parties who were now heading back to their cars – all pilgrims, all strangers, exchanging greetings and remarks on the marvellous weather and the extraordinary place.

The valley floor was quietening as we descended to it, except for the echoing croaks of circling ravens.

We found a grassy bank on which to pitch our tent close to where the river had once run through shingle, then was forced underground by the blockage of the fallen rocks. There was sufficient breeze to ward off the thousands of midges a party of Belgian mountaineers had warned us of.

We drank the beers and spread around us the treats we had carried including sweet Scottish strawberries, oatcakes with Manchego cheese. We made tea and later sampled the smoky taste of Macallan and Highland Park whiskies. And we revelled in the space, found bedtime reading in the wrinkled face of the stone and counted time only in the gullies etched by ice at least 12,000 years ago and by sunlight pinkly illuminating the west-facing ridge. Our bodies were still fresh enough to stroll along the rock-strewn valley for water, to stretch towards climbing moves on a boulder, and then with the dropping of the breeze, and the arrival of midge-squadrons, were persuaded towards horizontal.

No dusk was due any time soon in this northern summer, and it was not long before first light and the clamour of waking birds penetrated the flysheet, calling us outside to brew more tea. Dawn was now highlighting the west-facing wall of our vast, roofless room. There were no appointments, no news except for what the birds brought, and what the new light sang of. We were just ourselves, in bodily connection with land and sky. Then we gathered ourselves towards an onward climb after breakfast, up to the skyline and the snow, in a place just as lost and lonely as we wished it to be.

Later, against the tide of upcoming day-trippers from France and Connecticut, from a local outdoor centre for schools, we returned, down beside the icy plunge pools. This time we didn't resist them. I had no idea of the day of the week, nor cared. If the valley had hidden anything, it was myself, my own everyday routines and worries. Anxieties I was aware of before setting off were now thoroughly concealed from me.

As we reached the car, sweltering amidst the roar of tour buses still arriving and departing, we found that our long, languorous, energetic spell in the mountains had taken less than twenty-four hours. To follow in Stevenson's footsteps by taking to our feet and sleeping as part of the journey, agreeing like him to 'throw our clocks and watches over the housetop', is to be convinced when he declares that on a long summer's day, 'you will feel almost free'.

Weaving High Worlds

High on the blustery, wide-open slopes of Sgòr Gaoith, I was thrust deep into a tangly forest. Long twilled plumes of green rose up, tipped with slightly serrated, greyish filaments. Interlocked amongst them was a graveyard of giant antlers, each branching tine visibly hollow. Dense, and impenetrable, even for a knight seeking a sleeping beauty, how had such a thicket appeared on this Cairngorm roof, famous for its lack of trees?

What I was looking at was the tapestry of cushiony moss and lichen under my feet; an undulating spread I'd been bounding down. Dropping onto hands and knees, I'd delved my fingers luxuriously into it and smelt damp labrador and the far-north tundra. Venturing further, it transformed through the tiny portal of a magnifying lens handed to me by someone in our group. It was as revolutionary to the eye as the first time I snorkelled over a coral reef having only before marvelled at the sea's reflective surface. I was a child with a microscope; a wonder-struck astronaut seeing my planet from a wildly new perspective.

It was late May, and yet our small group had earlier gathered around a crop of grey lichen with brilliant red caps, 'Devil's matchsticks', striking up out of a nest of hailstones. Cloudberries flowered. Mountain azaleas tickled the grey slopes we climbed with pink pinpricks. We stood on the summit precipice and looked across a yawning gap. Deep within it Loch Einich lay darkly, and we bowed to Braeriach with its skirt of cloud, carved and corried and looming, as if close, in the moist air.

We were walking towards a corrie between here and Glenfeshie where Simone Kenyon's extraordinary dance piece animating Nan Shepherd's *The Living Mountain* would be performed. Three parties of walkers were to converge, each travelling with a mountain guide and the further expertise of a facilitator who knew land and botany.

I was excited by the tangle of syllables with which Jean named this floor tapestry. The word seemed fashioned by the spongy mesh of pale greens and greys itself, by its darker and damper depths. The surface was combed into a dry, feathery paleness that looked frosted from a distance as the great pelt rolled down the flank of the hill.

I asked Jean to put the name in my notebook.

'*Racomitrium,*' she wrote.

I was surprised to find it was a botanical term: Latin.

This was *Racomitrium* heath, a distinctive Alpine-Arctic groundcover on high, bare hills intertwining mosses, liverworts and lichens. Although, ironically, sheep will not eat it, the common name 'woolly fringe moss' is given to one of its principal constituents, *Racomitrium lanuginosum*, the one I'd seen with the pale, serrated tips. *Cladonia* lichens are in the mix too, and I learnt something I surely should have known sooner, that lichen, as well as being a powerful indicator of clean air, is a symbiotic collaboration between fungus and algae. Although the name *Cladonia* was new to me, it was familiar to my naked eye. I've always associated its multiple pale green branches with very different terrain: the underwater world of corals, or the bronchioles in lungs.

The plants making up this heath thread back 450 million years across the Scottish hills and lace it, inevitably, to the high, bare places of Norway, Sweden, Finland and Russia where reindeer still make their annual migrations, the hollow hairs of their pelts insulating them from harsh winters. Reindeers disappeared from Scotland 800 years ago, although since the 1950s they have been naturalising in the Cairngorms and feeding on hardy 'reindeer moss' (actually a lichen, *Cladonia rangiferina*). The only Sami word adopted into English, 'tundra', summons their hooves, pacing towards me across the tweedy hillside; incredible hooves, splayed to stop them sinking into snow, tendons clicking so they can locate each other in fog.

That day we saw a pair of dotterel, migratory waders smartly liveried with a black and white head and russet bib. Their other plumage disguises them as '*Racomitrium* heath' until they move in lurching bursts. At this time of year, the Cairngorm plateau is their breeding stronghold, where they feed on the heath's cranefly. The female is the more ornate of the pair and takes the lead in courtship, often then leaving the male to incubate the eggs.

The dotterel's name in Gaelic – *amadan mòintich* – means 'fool of the moss'. Its Latin name, *morinellus*, implies the same, and the common name comes etymologically from a similar meaning in Middle English; think dotard, dotty, Dodo, slurs arising from their trusting nature which makes it easy to get close, and in the past to trap this 'delicacy', now seriously threatened. A photo reveals three mottled eggs within a nest lined with grey-green *Cladonia uncialis* glowing amidst the plait of darker foliage. As magnification revealed, each antlerish tine is hollow, insulation allowing the eggs to be left unattended in low temperatures whilst the adult bird forages. The dotterel is no fool.

I walk in such places for the wide vistas, and to draw inspiration from being a minute human in a more-than-human place. But walking that day with a shared beat of feet and heave of lungs, with people happy to pool their knowledge, warped me a loom.

We flipped the scale, and we named things. Later, curiosity led me to add detail and I interleaved a weft. There was a new and peculiar pleasure for me in linking this close-looking, this understanding of the intertwining and co-dependency of separate species, with the feel in my mouth of Latin names.

And so a multi-dimensional world took shape from our short, shared pause in the landscape, evoking thickets of fairytale-ish, unfamiliar forest and a wise meshing of threads: Fungus and algae collaborating; cranefly supported by *Racomitrium* heath; dotterel reliant on cranefly for food and on *Cladonia uncialis* to insulate their nests. Finally, having come supernaturally close, I like to adjust the lens, step back and picture threads spooling out between the dotterel's breeding grounds on the Cairngorm plateau and a far-flung archipelago of reindeer-trodden tundra, mountain plateaux; weaving together high worlds.

Joyous Messengers

'Sundown on the high stonefields!'

My imagination soars into Arctic air up on the light-lashed Cairngorm plateau. In five words the poet has caught my imagination: Edwin Morgan, the 'Voice of Glasgow'.

And then down I go, swooping onto his reorientating second line, 'the darkening roofscape stirs', and I drop, as the poem's title suggests, into George Square. Cliffs loft around me – the General Post Office, the City Information Bureau, the City Chambers.

The square is 'alive with starlings'. It doesn't matter if I know nothing of these birds because he reveals their 'starling-ness' against the flash of a western window. In their collective, dark energy they cross it 'like a shower of arrows', then settle on wires as jet beads.

Light slicks these iridescent birds. I see the gleam of jet, but hear it too in the hiss of a couple of lines of shiny 's's. Then the starlings' clamour on those cliffs, their deafening warble, rises before they scatter again.

But it's what this gathering stirs in humans, first the pedestrians below and then those inside the cliff-dwellings, that really matter in *The Starlings in*

George Square. At first there's delight, especially in a wide-eyed boy to whom it will be a life-changer – he will never forget. But later they cause confusion in the Post Office where the word starling messes with Sterling, and in the City Chambers where the Lord Provost can't hear herself think. So begins the application of repellents and armoury against the avian mob: 'Send back the jungle'!

The spectacle of a vast murmuration of starlings knotting as one airborne gauze into a dragon, stretching to form a ship, and now whirlpooling away in a column, is one of our most breathtaking natural phenomena; up there with Northern Lights. But we're double-handed. 'I wonder if we really deserve starlings?' the poet asks as the humans claw George Square back with 'indignant orderliness' and the poem playfully makes its serious point.

So, are starlings affectionately-regarded wonders? Or are they invaders who steal crops, leave noxious waste and are simply too noisy? In 1949, by flocking with such density onto its hands, they stopped Big Ben. When Morgan wrote this poem in 1968, they were not always welcome in the cliff-ravines of cities and were treated as pests. Out of many regional variations, the 'star' in the common name, referring to the birds' white-flecked plumage, is retained in Staris in Shetland, Starnels in North East Dorset and Eurostars in Cape Town where they were a nineteenth-century introduction. Or they are Sheep Stares and Shebbies because they pick parasites from the backs of sheep. The names Wizards and Wheezers sing of their airy whistle. But then we have Greaseballs, Shitlegs and Stinkers.

With a relation in the myna bird, starlings might mimic a car-alarm or learn the exact note and into-nation of that man who, on returning from work, whistles from the street up to his partner to throw down their only key from a first-floor window. How many times a day is she summoned to find no one there? Perhaps they are too clever, not humble enough, getting one over on us like this.

In the 2020 RSPB Gardenwatch survey, the starling was the second most recorded bird, bely-ing its 80 per cent decline since the scheme began in 1979. The huge numbers of us who engaged with the 2021 survey reflect new enthusiasm for our avian neighbours during a year of more or less domestic confinement. They've been a constant, sometimes seeming in more boisterous voice due to our own stillness. Rather like poetry, they bring solace tucked amongst wing feathers, swoop delight into gardens, parks, and less crowded places as well as into our hearts when we choose to notice them; to *really* notice, as a poet must.

My own heart lightened in early February when I woke once again to birdsong in my garden and watched blackbirds in their flurried mating chase. Later that day I looked up into a roadside tree, its leafless branches punctuated by silhouetted birds as if they were notes on a stave. The tree itself seemed to vibrate with song; an orchestra suspended in the sky – one of those everyday miracles that stopped my feet and is available to all of us.

Whilst interest in the natural world can seem the preserve of middle-class white people in the countryside, birds give us a collective cause for wonder wherever we live. Like the 'wide-eyed' boy in the poem, Mark Lindo looked through a north-west London window as a child of Jamaican parents, and saw that birds were everywhere. Just as Morgan's childhood was short on household literature, Lindo grew up without bird enthusiasts at home or school, and so on his daily pre-breakfast watches, he gave birds his own names – starlings were 'mummy-birds' at first. Now known as the Urban Birder, he is a broadcaster, writer and educator with a mission to engage city folk around the world with the environment through the medium of birds. As he says, out of 620 species recorded in Britain, 95 per cent of them can be found in urban areas. And it's there that humans and birds are true cohabitees and may test our neighbourliness.

Morgan's play of black letter and white space often sings with mischief. Through penetrating observation and wordplay, his poetic output over a lifetime brings close attention to anything and everything, including the non-human. He steps beyond the City to spring a hyena bloody-fanged off the page, gives voice to the terrible loneliness of the Loch Ness Monster, maps Scotland in regional names for the chaffinch. An elegy for a poet lays out the qualities of Basil Bunting against avian buntings in 'A Trace of Wings'. But the non-human more often animates his city. He coaxes wolves onto Blythswood Hill, asking for 'a little wildness please'; a gull at his window unnerves, stamping and assessing him through the glass. And then we have the 'confused sweetness' of the starlings.

They are a fine match, poet and bird: songster and magician, mimic and tease, making minds dance, hearts soar, taking us on linguistic adventures and making us ask how we should live together.

Street Play in Edinburgh

For over four years in the early 1990s, I lived near Stirling, commuting to work in Edinburgh by train. I walked a short distance through the convulsions of the Old Town from Waverley Station to a small close off the Canongate. I don't need to labour the magic of Edinburgh as a city to explore on foot, including as it does a volcano to climb, wheeling gulls and views to the Forth. The National Library of Scotland houses eight acres of books in storeys climbing between two streets stacked one above the other.

In some cities 'enchantment engineers' design temporary illusions for pedestrians to experience as part of their journey – gardens, benches, special pathways or artworks. But such interventions are hardly needed in Edinburgh where there is abundant evidence of past lives and opportunities for improvisation. Pedestrians can navigate the Old Town by statues, pubs and remarkable buildings; there are pavements for a pacing rhythm, but also car-free ways, gaits, closes, stairs that invite us to saunter, shamble, strut or turn back on ourselves.

But I was intent on getting to work. My train arrived at 8.48 and I hurried to be seated at my desk for 9.00am, so I chose the 'stride' and the most direct route. On drowsed arrival at Waverley,

I stepped into greenish light splashed through thirteen acres of mossy, cantilevered glass. I danced a criss-cross quickstep on the esplanade, fan-tailing from the ticket barrier with my fellow passengers, dodging on-comers, making a bee-line for paths up and out. We were chased by jarring sounds: warped announcements, whistles, coffee machines, taxi rattle, clickety-clack heels and the rumble of wheeled cases. I doubt we even noticed, in this gorge separating the Old Town from the New, the ghostly lapping at our ankles of the loch and sewer which were drained to make way for railway tracks.

I climbed up from Waverley's depths onto Market Street, ready to head into the stacks of the old town cliff, an un-mappable wilderness to the south. Here, according to Robert Louis Stevenson in the 1870s, 'houses sprang up storey after storey, neighbour mounting upon neighbour's shoulder, as in some Black Hole of Calcutta, until the population slept fourteen or fifteen deep in a vertical direction.'

The crowd I was part of divided three ways here. The most committed crossed Market Street and sprang up steeply-stepped Fleshmarket Close. Those less brave turned right. But I was carried along with the group striding left, the mountains and valleys of Waverley's glass roof now stretching away below us. Our heads snatched back over our shoulders, seeking a gap in the traffic to cross towards the curve of Jeffrey Street which would take us to the Royal Mile. We didn't stop and wait.

Somewhere under North Bridge, one person led the step off the pavement, and as if by agreement the rest of us followed in a scattered arc. We were brave jaywalkers between buses, taxis, the silent swipe past of cycles. I've discovered since that there's an anthropological term for this. 'Togethering' is when traffic-dominated pedestrians are encouraged by each other to move as one body. And yet we didn't speak, avoided each other's eyes, didn't admit at all that we were 'together'.

Here under North Bridge, three parallel universes hover on the same coordinate offering different experiences. This was Waverley's over-world but we traversed the hotel underworld where broken glass was expelled, leaving splinters underfoot. We slalomed between empty tomato boxes piled for collection and metal beer kegs clanging down from trucks. The grand hotels – the Carlton, the Scotsman – turn their backs onto Market Street, offering smart doorways for their guests on the street above.

It was also where white vans lined up. Flasks lay on dashboards. Newspapers slashed red letters against the glass: *The Daily Record*. Men slept in the seats with folded arms, perhaps dreaming. Did I ever ask myself of what?

Jeffrey Street – a gentle traffic-filled slope between Market Street and the High Street – was the safe, direct route. It seems to me now that the steeper, the narrower, the more convoluted the way through the precipice of the Old Town, the more exposure we have to goblin and ghost. Out of the back doors of businesses on dark closes boxes of rotten fruit and wilting bouquets were chucked. Off-duty workers lurked there with cigarettes. There were 'NO FLY POSTING' notices on newly painted walls, but also graffiti. The clap of pigeons' wings was amplified between high cliffs.

I might have climbed, breathless, past smashed windows, reading mottos in Scots and Latin above doorways – 'He who tholes overcomes', '*Spes Altera Vitae* 1590' (Hope of another life) – then climbed ever-narrowing steps until I burst through a tunnel onto the High Street to be ambushed by bagpipe music, tour guides and portrait artists, tourists drifting with maps and guides.

An alternative way was offered by the Scotsman Steps, whose doorway we passed close to those hotel backyards. Once under a sylvan archway of curli-cued oak leaves, I could have spiralled up through a stone column. In those days before its marble-make-over by artist Martin Creed, I would have passed smokers and last night's vomit piles. At each turn an arched window gave views of Market Street, the old Grammar School on the hill, Waverley Station, all tipping wildly in perspective as I gained height. Dizzied by spinning I'd be pushed out into sudden light and air on North Bridge with a long view to the sea. A different world.

There were not only different routes I could have tried, but different *ways* of walking. What if I had walked my usual route at the pace of a toddler, or occasionally stopped and closed my eyes to listen, or chosen my route by the toss of a dice at each corner – might I have had a richer experience of commuting?

But instead I carried on along Jeffrey Street on my blinkered mission without a second thought as to who Jeffrey was, past the posh boutiques and tapas bars, to a busy cobble-purred crossroads. Each corner spilled with pedestrians impatient for their turn, stepping out and back, waiting or not waiting for the green man at the crossing before plunging on. Perhaps sometimes I glanced across at The World's End pub, the boundary of two burghs, a landmark infamous for the destiny of two girls.

I turned left down the Canongate towards work. Under the high escarpment of one of the Old Town's multi-storey 'lands', I took a tunnel called Old Playhouse Close. If I'd looked up, a sign above the gated entrance tells that it, 'Led to a theatre and hall where from 1747 to 1769 famous actors, actresses and singers performed. Home's 'Douglas' was first staged here in 1756.' But I was intent on arriving on time for my non-play in the Playhouse. In retrospect I seem to have guarded myself from all the enchantment that this square kilometre of Edinburgh might have offered. I've counted over twenty closes that were on my route, like creeks or tributaries off a main watercourse. Each might have offered me diversion, in both senses of the word – a turning away, and an entertainment.

In August people scurry between Festival venues or take time to stroll, to drift, to explore Edinburgh. Those trying to go about their ordinary business have to become expert at the 'Do-Si-Do' dance of city movement, slipping through a wall of walkers with a kink of the hips and a twist of the shoulders. We are birds in flight, continuously adjusting to the currents of the streets. Even so, pavement rage is not unknown amongst those who are heads-down and purposeful, perhaps longing for the un-peopled hills.

I'd wondered if being the daughter of a great Victorian alpinist had helped make Virginia Woolf into a writer. Presumably walking was part of family life, and the mountains might have given her space to dream. But it wasn't wild places that excited her. 'How could I think mountains and climbing romantic?' she apparently asked. 'Wasn't I brought up with alpenstocks in my nursery, and a raised map of the Alps showing every peak my father had climbed? Of course London and the marshes are the places I like best.' Like Thomas Hardy and Charles Dickens who walked themselves into a thorough knowledge of London and its people, and thus into imaginative realms of fiction, she took to the streets.

In her 1927 essay 'Street Haunting: A London Adventure', Woolf wrote of going out to buy a pencil and digressing well beyond her errand, putting on 'for a few minutes the bodies and minds of others'. She observes, overhears, but maintains her distance: 'One could become a washerwoman, a publican, a street singer. And what greater delight and wonder can there be than to leave the straight lines of personality and deviate into those footpaths that lead beneath brambles and thick tree trunks into the heart of the forest where live those wild beasts, our fellow men?'

Walking with imaginations alert might turn into an act of empathy or lead to a sense of belonging to a place. In Michelle de Krestner's novel *Questions of Travel*, a refugee arriving in an Australian city gives his days up to walking and finds that the process is 'porous'. He comes to know and understand the place.

For fiction writers, every passing face is a mystery. What's the story behind that overhead snatch of conversation and its promise: *'I said I'd do it.*

Did it twice actually.'? Why is a single child's shoe lying on an empty table on the High Street? What prompted the scaffolder in a white suit to perform a small dance for his laughing workmates as they leant against their van on a coffee break? Each one begs an invention, the simple question, 'What if?' for a story to take flight.

City walking allows a distance from others which excites imagination. Janet Cardiff, a Canadian artist who has exhibited at the Fruitmarket Gallery, is famous for her site-specific audio-walks in which the headset guides the walker's observations whilst delivering a narrative about a character taking the same route. The walker has two experiences of a place at once. Janet Cardiff herself says: 'A lone walker is both present and detached from the world around, more than an audience, but less than a participant.' This state is fertile ground for the imagination.

Richard Long, a land artist whose work is closely connected with walking, says: 'Our bodies are elemental: we are animals, we make marks, we leave traces, we leave footprints.' On the earth paths I follow around my home in Perthshire, I love the sense that I personally know some of the people whose repeated dog-walk or route to a pony has initiated a way through summer undergrowth. Others like me follow it, adding to the wear so that a path becomes established.

In walking Edinburgh's streets now, I stop sometimes to examine steps halfway up Fleshmarket Close. Each one is hollowed with wear, but one of them drops deeper on its left-hand side. I ponder the story behind it. What obstacle on its right side forced millions of footfalls over centuries into the preference recorded here?

As for memory-traces from my own repeated commuter route, I find them vanished, evaporated, rubbed quite away. The streets don't remember or recall me. I might as well have diverted. I realise now that a walk to work doesn't have to be head-down, fast-paced oblivion. It could be a time for noticing, to be playful. It could be altered by leaving home extra-early and walking the bus route normally dozed through, this time noticing and discovering the places passed.

If I had my job again in Old Playhouse Close, I would do what it demands and play with my twelve-minute walk from Waverley. And if I am a little late? So what?

'Today I Stand in a Field and Shout'

It's one of those damp, chill November days in July. The cycle twelve miles south from Aberfeldy to Corbenic Camphill Community is half taken up with the winding climb crossing the hills between two valleys. As I puff upwards I mentally take my hat off to Jon Plunkett, poet and founder of the Corbenic Poetry Path, who cycles this journey to work every day (albeit with a little battery assistance). After the summit at Loch na Creige, I soar through grouse moor, spruce plantations, windfarms, freewheeling down into Strath Braan and along the green and glittering ribbon it sashays between scratchy hills, running east towards Birnam and Dunkeld. Down here woodland rolls into hollows and contented cows munch. Because it is actually July, the verges explode in great, wet heads of cow parsley and meadowsweet, splashes of foxglove colour, willow-herb. The corridor is scented by sappy bracken.

I set out on Corbenic's poetry path enjoying the sense that I am 'beating the bounds' of the 50-acre estate. Without intruding on those who live here, I look over my left shoulder onto varied cameos of Perthshire countryside – pasture, open hillside, native woodland and wild river – whilst on my right,

I glimpse a tractor at work, chickens pecking in a field, a pony-riding lesson going on, and amidst fresh sawdust, beehive-shaped piles of chopped logs waiting to warm a hearth. Voices mark the criss-crossing of ways between home and work.

Corbenic is a community for adults with learning disabilities where creative activity is prioritised through music, stories and the crafting of things: loaves of bread, pottery, furniture and candles, all sold in their shop and café in Dunkeld, four miles away. There is also a small farm, the land and animals tended in a way that shows the many hands at work and low levels of mechanisation.

Opened in June 2015 following development over three years or so, the poetry path was a new way for residents to help create something, and to enjoy their home on foot. Up to fifty volunteers a day also gave their time, including staff from Scottish and Southern Energy through a company volunteering scheme. It follows that many people are now proud of the result.

I set off into midgey drizzle on the 3km (2 mile) walk. 'It is good to stand in a field and shout', Jim Carruth's poem soon declares from its beautifully carved stone slab, the word 'shout' repeated three large times so I am not in doubt. This joyous, raucous, rhythmic poem invites me back to childhood. It seems to define this place where residents can enjoy being in the landscape, secure within boundaries and an expectation of sharing, yet free to express themselves.

With renewed energy I bound on. The path is well-made, lined sometimes with birch logs, sometimes with stone. Sometimes decking is suspended over a bog. Later there are more poems carved, as Jim Carruth's, by artisan stone-carver and staff member Martin Reilly but the approach to materials is playful and varied. Ron Butlin's poem 'Before the Program Starts' appears under gel on the top of a blue marker post. Nearby a television screen is fixed into a dry-stone dyke and a remote control left handily on a stump. I know now not to expect uniformity.

The path jinks on between birch trees, inviting me onwards around a far bend into what looks like a pool of light. What will be next? It's nineteen words from Kenneth Steven laid out in reverse order along the path. The final word 'island' is met first, but to read the whole line I walk to the top and then return nine paces. It's about the hurry in our lives, so dwelling here makes sense. And there it is at the end: '...find an island' – a discovery made for the second time.

In the dark of a conifer plantation, knee deep in grass, there's a small thrill between spotting a blue post and finding the poem it marks. At the forest edge a pile of logs three-deep is silhouetted against the growing brightness of the fields and hills beyond. When my eyes adjust I see words carved into slate slicing through the middle layer. 'Time has taught the uses of silence': a line from a Sally Evans poem. As well as the surprise of the physical discovery, 'silence' makes a nice reply, ten minutes on, to 'shout'. But it also resonates with what I'm looking at: the high hills and cleft of Glen Quaich to our west, where in the 19th century repeated clearances silenced the valley.

Patricia Ace's poem responding to the mossy gable ends of a ruined croft is etched on a sheet of glass, its horizon a jagged mountain range. It's suspended high so that as you walk, the words appear and vanish, appear and vanish depending on the light and landscape behind. Sometimes the words hang in the clouds, sometimes against stone walls. Glimpsed singly or in small groups they make sense of the context: 'etched', 'work and weather', 'distant lives'.

Nature and the elements edit the pieces. Wind has drifted twigs across some of Kenneth Steven's words. Rain-wet stone is sometimes harder to read. Or easier. Next to the water-lily lochan at the highest point of the walk, and under the crag where the hill ground is starting to purple with ling, Morgan Downie's poem 'Casting' invokes geese, buzzards, wagtails, grouse. Its fine timber 'page' has been amended. Two long white lines of bird shit run down across the words.

'Today I Stand in a Field and Shout'

The walk comprises thirty-two poems by nineteen poets, some locally based, most known Scotland-wide, and many of them poets of the rural with an affinity to the land. Some of the poems or lines were selected by Jon Plunkett for particular locations. Some poets visited the site and responded to a chosen corner. The creativity that's gone into the installations themselves, and into their positioning, adds to the playful nature of the whole experience.

A poem by Tim Turnbull looks east across a dyke to fields sloping steeply towards Craig Laggan, and refers to a 'gateway to another world'. A few paces on, with that line still echoing, I find it incarnate in a cast-iron gate opening onto the same view.

'When I said you should/grab the bull by the horns/I thought you would understand'. A snort and scuffle interrupt this reading of Jon Plunkett's poem 'Lost in Translation'. A bullock stands just beyond the wall ahead, nose raised towards me.

Dropping down on a winding path between mature birch trees, thickets of bracken and foxglove, I'm wondering what will come next, when Margaret Gillies Brown's 'The Inner Citadel' arrives in the centre of the path, with its journey 'into the dark interior/down, down, down'.

An iteration begins: poem with poem, poem against setting, chimes and rhymes. I'm now aware of walking a three-dimensional anthology.

Down through a mossy corridor between rho-
dodendron; down to the river, with the rain on
again, closed in by dark and drip, fern and moss,
and the river's gurgle, there's a place to sit and have
a fire and a feeling of an end approaching. It's here
that John Glenday's poem 'The River' provides the
emotional crux of this anthology for me, with its
resistance to endings, and a possibility of 'the river
never quite reaching the sea'. The Braan swings
around a bend making a deep pool that's prickled
by rain, then slicked by brief sun. It tumbles away
over stone towards the Tay and thus to the sea, as if
in contradiction. I stand there for some time, shake
off a shiver not only brought about by the chill,
then climb back towards the start of the walk, closing the circle.

After I stop for a sandwich, the sun comes out
and I can't help starting the walk again, the same
impulse as returning to the first pages of a book
after a satisfying resolution. I discover a poem I
missed the first time and things look slightly different. Under sunlight the patchwork of grouse moor
on the hills is revealed more starkly, the purpling
spread of ling more pronounced.

This slow walk syncopated with 'poem stations'
will be different and bring a new pleasure each time
I visit. I'm going to enjoy the editing style of different seasons: Autumn's cut determined by the fall of

leaves; winter's by snow; spring's by the distracting scent of wild garlic down on the flood-eaten river banks. Or I'll come at different times of day; I'll creep up on Sally Evans' log pile at dawn when the words will be lit from the east. Sometimes there'll be shouting, sometimes silence.

I leave Corbenic with a spring in my step (or in my pedals) as if now, with my poetry-expanded heart and lungs full of fresh air, I feel gloriously free to stand in a field and shout.

A Bubbling Immediacy

I like to imagine the blether that took place between Jessie Kesson and Nan Shepherd on an early spring day in 1941 when they found themselves sitting face-to-face on a train travelling from Inverurie towards Elgin. When she stumbled aboard, Kesson saw that her carriage companion was to be a 'lady'. Married to a simple cottar herself, she would be considered a 'wifie'. Despite their fundamental differences, she blurted out the morning's news of the death of a favourite poet 'Hamewith', or Charles Murray, who wrote in Doric. The news found common ground and pitched the two women into an encounter with lasting consequences.

According to Kesson, they 'tired the sun with talking'. Their backgrounds could not have been more different, and yet they shared a passion for the woods and hills that passed by the window of their carriage, and a love of words and literature. Kesson, who had made a small but promising start in writing by that time, often attributed her further determination to this chance meeting. Shepherd encouraged her to enter a short story competition, which she subsequently won.

I picture them leaning towards each other, illuminated by flashes of spring sunlight between Scots pine, noting the wood anemones spilling down the banks next to the tracks, catching at each other's joys, so that Shepherd later remarked on Kesson's 'life gushing out in all sorts of ways'. At the end of the journey, a strawberry-coloured silk headscarf passed from Shepherd to Kesson as a memento of the encounter and a lifelong literary friendship began. It led indirectly to Kesson's distinctive voice being caught between the pages of a book seventeen years later: *The White Bird Passes*.

In their sharing of Doric words, surely they must have lingered over one in particular. Kesson in this, her first novel, as well as in her other works, vividly animates the condition of the *ootlin* – the Aberdeenshire word she uses for 'queer folk who were "out" and who, perversely enough, never had any desire to be "in"'. Towards the end of the novel, an authority figure puzzles over Janie, the young narrator, finding her 'far too knowing for [her] years' whilst fearing that she will soon 'find the world a tough place'. This paradox, reiterated by others, characterises a girl who may have witnessed too much of adult confusions, but arrives on the page with an acute but naive sensitivity. Simultaneously old and young, sharply observant and articulate on the agonies of loss and absence, she makes the perfect narrator.

Janie can be both solitary and gregarious, is at

ease in the natural world and yet has an affinity with 'ne'er-do-weels', the disadvantaged and oppressed. These tensions and paradoxes are perhaps the axis of the novel's magic, opposing the eight-year-old (and latterly sixteen-year-old) Janie's playfulness and occasional fearful withdrawal into solitary thought and imagination, with a surprising revelry in the bawdy wit, curses and sensory mayhem of the Elgin lane that is her childhood home.

The novel reveals the particularity of lives that have conventionally remained untold and is thus a valuable document of social history. However, it is also charged with universal emotion and eloquently filtered through a child's imagination. The fine line Kesson's work treads between autobiography and fiction, so sensitively and fully explored in Isobel Murray's *Jessie Kesson: Writing Her Life*, is inescapable here. The experience of growing up in the 1920s in an Elgin slum, the absent father and the Skene orphanage are undoubtedly drawn from Kesson's own life, material she re-trod both on the page and in her writing for radio. But what matters in a reading of *White Bird* is not identifying what was selected from life, what was omitted or invented, but its powerful sense of authenticity. It is candid and deeply felt, yet humorous, and it dances off the page with its sheer love of language.

A Bubbling Immediacy

White Bird was published in hardback in 1958, but it wasn't until Michael Radford's BBC film in 1980 that it received the acclaim it deserved and appeared in paperback. Along with the many good reviews on initial publication, an accusation was made by *The Daily Record and Mail*: 'Daughter Shows No Shame'. This alluded to the portrayal in the novel of the mother's small-time prostitution and child neglect that attracted the attention of the 'cruelty man', thought to be autobiographical.

Arguably, rather than a slur on a mother, it can be read as a love letter. At home in the claustrophobic lane, Janie's mother is preoccupied and elusive and the narrative is taut with fear of her death. But when mother and daughter leave the lane and walk five miles through countryside to visit her grandmother, it explodes into a sense of space and green, of joy and liberty. Their poetic naming of the flowers, the vitality of scent, song and story elevate their intimacy. Such moments with the beloved mother who 'saw a legend in the canna flowers and a plough amongst the stars' are luminous almost because of their rarity. As Janie says, such fleeting times 'more than made up for the other things lacking in their relationship' and are coupled with the child's fierce sense of protection and responsibility at moments of her mother's vulnerability. There is also an adult sense of gratitude: 'I would myself be blind now, if she had never lent me her eyes'.

Kesson transformed personal hardship into a story of beauty, enchantment and humour, told with the 'bubbling immediacy' that Nan Shepherd remarked on in her 1958 review. When she gives us Janie, 'just walking along watching the mists steam from the seams of the Cairngorms,' or she observes the *peesie* (lapwing) 'weeping its grief across the stubble field', a vein pulses between the inner life of a vivacious child and a powerful sense of place. Her words skewer the poignancy of joy or heartbreak.

Kesson braved a barrier of class and education when she initiated that encounter on the train in 1941 and connected by chance with a writer who also found landscape and self inseparable and focused on small, northern communities. In a sense, she never returned to the margins and she remained courageous. Perhaps Janie's frustrated cry – 'I want to write poetry. Great poetry!' – was indeed Kesson's own at that particular crossroads in her life. Thankfully, now that we have passed the centenary of the year of her birth (1916), the spirit that is embodied in her words and her marvellous story lives on.

Borrowed Boots

In late May 2016 I arrived in Exeter wearing my own well-worn boots and set off on a walk to Teignmouth my parents had taken some sixty-seven years earlier. I was tiptoeing over other memories stretching back to the scent of the Somme on my grandfather's boots and my mother's childhood and youth in Exeter. I had my own memories of the area too, having visited my grandparents as a child and come to live here between 1979 and 1990, first as a student and then during my early years of employment.

My mother's account below suggests that they started climbing towards Haldon Hill somewhere close to Exeter. At that time the hillside was free of the spaghetti snarls of the M5 and A38. She was unable to recall their route so I invented my own, at first keeping low along the canal and Exe estuary south to Powderham Castle. It turned out that this first leg was rich with my own memories, punctuated by two pubs I often went to at Double Locks and Turf Locks, where I'd also tied up in various boats on the way to sail out to wider waters. Having set off in the afternoon, I broke my journey overnight near the village of Kenton, leaving the climb up to the great ridge of Haldon to the south for the next morning.

Writing Landscape

For as long as I can remember I'd thought of
my mother as a walker and as a painter, but I'd
never considered her a writer even though she won
a poetry competition when I was a teenager. And
I'd never heard before about this walk taken after
meeting my father at Oxford until I read her story
anthologised in *Word Play*, which was published by
the Penzance Ladies' Book Club as a fundraiser for
the Morrab Library in 2006.

*'But these are the only shoes I have,' I said. Shoes
were important. Five years after the war ended,
everything I possessed was important: one dress,
one coat, one two-piece suit, one pair of slacks cut
down from my aunt's Land Army dungarees,
some stockings, and a pair of tidy shoes.*

*Richard and I had come down from our
respective colleges to our Exeter homes for the
Easter vacation. We were at his parents' house,
planning our first major expedition – our first
whole day together. We were going to walk over the
ridge of the Haldon Hills and down to the coast
at Teignmouth, staying off roads where we could.
But I had no boots, only these thin-soled shoes.*

*'Hang on a moment, what size are you?' asked
his father, and disappeared. He came back with
his army boots from the war before last. He was a
smallish man, and they were my size.*

He put them down in front of me. I looked at them, set side by side on the pastel carpet. Gleaming with ancient spit and polish, they had bent into comfortable shapes and then become gnarled leather sculptures after years in a cupboard. They had about them an air of containment, of secrets – much like their owner. It seemed as though they were still imbued with molecules of the Somme. After a moment I ventured to slide my feet into their dark mouths. If I wore thick socks, they would do.

We met next day with our knapsacks and thermoses, crossed the Exe valley and started to climb. It was a fine April day, full of windy light. There had been rain overnight, which gave everything a washed brightness. Trees were hazy with fresh green, and primroses studded the high hedges. We walked deep-sunk lanes past cob-walled farms shouldered in among trees. Red Devons lowed as they were chivvied from a yard: 'Come up Beauty, Daisy, Cherry'. At every farm, battered silvery churns stood by the gate.

Our path cut across meadows of wet glossy grass and buttercups, which bucked in the wind. It ran along margins of barley fields where new pale green bayonets stabbed up through dull crimson earth. We tore our way past last year's wiry brambles, and climbed high stiles, where I made sure to jump into his arms.

Near the top we looked back at Exeter. The pale cathedral stood out above the bombed city, which from a distance appeared undamaged. On the summit we celebrated with sandwiches and Camp coffee. Through the trees we looked south to the sea, a distant glimmer of hammered tin.

On the long tramp down, I was more and more comfortable in the boots, but Richard had begun to limp. We rested and talked to a farmer, who led a young horse. The horse danced uneasily beside him, its ears mobile with anxiety. The hedges around us were newlylaid, saplings half severed and woven into horizontal wickerwork along the banks.

Late in the afternoon we arrived in Teignmouth, tired but triumphant, and in Richard's case, lame. Joggling together on the back seat of the bus home, we measured our walk on the map: seventeen miles.

I looked down at the boots, which had gradually warmed and softened to clasp the ankles of a green girl. They had been washed by rainy grass and bombarded with soft yellow explosions of buttercup pollen. They had withstood barbed-wire brambles and their soles now carried a sticky cake of Devon soil, the colour of blood.

We arrived back aching, warm and happy, and stood on the carpet in our stockinged feet, grinning. My future father-in-law looked up from his evening paper.

'Well,' he said to his son, 'can she walk?'

The landscape I walked into from Kenton the next morning was recognisable from my mother's description. Like my parents, I tried to avoid tarmac as much as possible and soon found myself on a web of small lanes, deep-sunk bridleways and permissive paths which sometimes tunnelled through trees towards a porthole of light within which a thatched roof might be framed.

Like them, I was walking after a night's rain and there was a sense of dank greenness, the soil a deep, clotty red. The verges were effervescent with grasses, bluebells, forget-me-nots, pink and white campions, high pillars of foxglove. I had to excavate some of the names from the silt of memory – names that had been spoken aloud by my mother on our many family walks when I was a child: pimpernel, angelica, speedwell.

Halfway up the hill I met a Norwegian man with his dog and explained why I was wandering the lanes.

'An exciting walk!' he said, smiling broadly before walking on towards his morning coffee.

By contrast my B&B host had stopped wiping a table and looked up when I told him my route.

'Is there something bad about it?' I asked.

'Not as long as you like hills,' he said. 'There's a 20 per cent gradient near the top. Good luck.'

I had two Ordnance Survey maps with me: a cloth one from 1946 – probably the one my parents carried – and the pink-jacketed 1974 version I used when I lived here. The names I read from the maps and on signposts left no doubt where I was. 'Clumpit Lane' could be nowhere but in Devon, and as I walked upwards, the thrill of being back in this half-familiar landscape matched the party-spirit of the late Spring day.

I edged upwards through dense oak woodlands marked on the map as 'Haydon Common'. Lichen-tendrilled branches danced from enormous trunks, pheasants cackled and birdsong echoed as though the woodland was sealed with a roof. At a three-way junction an old black and white 'lighthouse-style' road marker had lost all three of its direction posts, but the maps led me along a deeply-furrowed bridleway south-west, rising steeply towards Great Haldon. A ruckle of large pink-white stones drew a dim line along its centre.

There was a wet, woody scent. Through gaps in the deep, dark banks and hedges, buttercup-hazed meadows glinted, carrying seated brown cows. And then I was sprung out onto a small road that runs the Haldon spine, surprised to pass a 'Huskies Exercise Area'.

A man getting a large Alsatian out of his car asked me: 'Have you got a Mac?'

He stretched the last word, meaning a raincoat, into two syllables as my grandmother would have done.

He continued: 'They just said on the radio: it's raining from one o'clock.'

Delivering this news seemed to fill him with glee. I looked at my watch. There was about half an hour to go.

I had lunch at the edge of the steep escarpment at Mamhead, the highest point. The view below was hazy and I could only distinguish the widening end of the estuary and the sea beyond by faint, white, inshore stripes. I wondered what had filled my parents' sandwiches and whether they were carried in the same canvas knapsack I'd inherited and used for my earliest independent walking.

As I dropped steeply, first on tarmac and then on sticky-underfoot bridleways that skirted Luscombe Castle, the haze began to lift and I plunged back into warm sunshine. (Ba to you Mr 'Ma-ac', I thought). For some reason I had imagined it would be downhill all the way to Teignmouth. I'd forgotten how the miniature nature of this landscape belies the surprising challenges of its gradients. It was a rollercoaster of tight-coombed valleys. The air was pollen-rich. A line of ducks crossed the road at a shallow ford. The earth dried back to pink.

Crossing Dawlish Water, I was tempted to follow it into the town, to the coast. I recalled the many afternoons spent sitting on benches in the gardens beside the river with my grandmother, watching the ducks. But I was tiring now and didn't divert.

At last I came out onto the headland above Teignmouth. Everything was glittering below. The railway line curved around the coast towards faint cliffs. A clear trajectory led downhill to the seafront; a swaying path between high oaks. I doubt cream teas were on offer to my parents so I had one for them, gazing along the beach to a rickety pier. Legs dissolving in haze, it appeared to levitate.

I assume my mother passed the Cracknells' 'Can she walk?' test with flying colours: she married my father the following year. Her own parents were pioneers of the walking holiday, appearing in photos from the late 1920s on various coastal headlands, each carrying a small canvas rucksack. My mother continued the tradition with us, championing walks for brambling and flower-spotting, an infamous summiting of Snowdon in a blizzard, and countless coastal walks in Cornwall accompanied by a picnic basket.

On Haldon Hill I had stopped to talk to two women laced together by the leads of four large dogs. They seemed thrilled by the idea of my walk and who had inspired it. They took a photo of me and we stood chatting and smiling at each other for some time before parting ways.

Borrowed Boots

Like them, I was in no doubt who my 'boots' had come from and perhaps, I now realise, from where I got my pen.

The Indoor Outdoor Writer

This morning I walked the Birks of Aberfeldy before settling down to work. It was a bright, chill late April morning. Although I'd suffered sunburn the previous week, this morning the frost nipped at my fingers and snow had settled low on surrounding hills.

Despite its familiarity, the place still offers fresh and unexpected observations. With its climb up a woodland ravine to an impressive waterfall, it gives me a good physical workout as well as being a route layered with previous footfall invoking story and memory. I may walk it early in the morning, as today, or in the dopey hour after lunch, or to celebrate the end of the working day.

From Aberfeldy's streets and neat gardens and then a path narrowing through picnic tables, I walked towards something more elemental. Low down in the dank, deep places where the burn chitters, tree trunks and boulders were cling-wrapped in moss, luminous in the low light but dry to the touch like warm animal coats. Whilst the woodland remained mainly skeletal, the first slight flush of green crowned the maroon brush of the birch trees high above. Last year's crisp golden bracken, flattened by the winter gales and snow, carried over it a drift of wood anemones, their pale bell-flowers twitched by breezes. There were joyful pockets of primrose and violet and wild garlic leaves in lush clumps on the banks of the burn, their scent hooting: 'Spring!'

Motion lubricates my writing. My novel *Call of the Undertow* was written whilst repeatedly walking the beach and dunes at Dunnet Bay and cycling the Caithness lanes that radiate from it. In this way my characters got themselves entangled with local stories, geographical features, storms and sunsets. I didn't actually write it in motion but the ideas came with the visceral sensations of that place, got scribbled down on the move and later materialised into scenes.

I started writing *Doubling Back*, my first serious foray into non-fiction, partly because my fiction writing was becoming so physically embodied in places and landscapes. If I had to walk to write, why not write *about* some walking journeys which fascinated me because of the weight of memory-mud they left clinging to my boots? After setting off in 2007, I quickly walked up a full-length manuscript of ten journeys. Although it was shortlisted for the Robin Jenkins Award for Environmental Writing in 2009, it wasn't ready to be published until May 2014. This tells another story, not of additional walks or journeys re-trodden, but of the long and convoluted process of revising and restructuring.

This isn't a complaint about revision; each new circuit of an essay allows me to relive the journey and savour again the details in a way that a mental act of recall would not evoke so vividly. But for me, the time taken to batter and hone an essay into a readable shape takes many times the length of the experience itself. And that's not to mention the work in making essays cohabit and iterate within a meaningful-feeling book.

Non-writing friends and acquaintances picture me stomping across moors, up hills, following drove roads and poetry-paths as my 'normal' occupation. Conversely I picture myself mostly developing cramped shoulders and sciatic pain from sitting still too much and missing out on all the outdoor fun others are having. What cruel irony! Far from keeping me out of doors and active, getting *Doubling Back* fit for publication largely kept me at a desk (admittedly a month of it in the delightful setting of Lavigny International Writers' Retreat in Switzerland).

Fortunately for this oh-to-be-outdoors writer who spends so much of her time staring wistfully out of the window, the famous hour-long walk a stone's throw from my home has shown itself able to 'stand in' for some of the impulses which originally moved my pen. The walk resuscitates me, reminds me of moving in that big outdoors and clicks things back into perspective. It's not that my regular visits are a substitute for a fifteen-day walk along a drove road or the pursuit of my long-dead father up a white Alpine slope. But it returns me to the rhythms of walking, the breath and pulse and meaning found in the buds about to spring open, or an old road trailing a faint depression across a hillside. During rewriting, such reminders regrounded me in those stories. This local path has been a companion and memory-bank and vehicle, exercising my imagination and my emotions as well as my body.

If I've been at my desk, I nearly always need to lighten up. This morning, two red squirrels shimmied at speed up dual-carriageway tree trunks, inviting me to look up into the high canopy and making me smile. A small face peered over a branch as if ready to pelt me with victor's nuts. If I need to reconnect to humanity, there are nearly always other walkers, rarely passed without a greeting or an exclamation of joy or weariness. And there is Robert Burns and his song to remind me of the role of a writer. His statue has been sitting in a clearing since 1998, composing on the spot with notebook in hand. As I reached him this morning, I saw that since I passed him the day before, someone had filled the gap made by his long-ago-stolen pencil with a small twig.

As I continued on the well-trodden path, my cares started to fall back with the accompanying chuckle of the burn and the birds. My body clicked into its two-time rhythm, the breath flowed in and out, and thoughts meandered between inner land-scapes and actual observation. Between the uneasy presence of two owls in a short story I'm revising that aren't sure why they are there and young beech leaves that are backlit almost translucent yellow. It brings me back to what generates the words, what sparks the imagination.

Higher up the path, I climbed out of the dark crevice and, after the zigzagging tiers of steps came a reminder that despite the car park, and the signs warning about trips and slips, this is still a place at nature's mercy. Over the winter, burns pouring down the steep walls of the ravine have gouged new ways with their white water, shifted rocks, dumped tan-gled branches between boulders. Toppled trees hung with lichen were angled across gaps in the foliage.

After the bridge crossing the waterfall I came to a summit of sorts, and broke out of the trees to a mountain-cold blast of wind from the West. It's high enough here, at nearly 300 metres (1,000 feet), to make me feel lifted out of the everyday world, shown a more encompassing perspective; the sort so valued by mountaineers and pilgrims. And I looked into the western hills and imagined setting off through the gaps between them carrying a full backpack and a map. I breathed deeply. Schiehallion soared, white and sharp on a long, jagged horizon, and the Tay Valley sliced across my view below with its mixture of wild and tame, pylons reminding me of power generation and its implication of home, roads that take me away from here. I know that down there oystercatchers are piping again by the river and in one of the houses in the town my worries and deadlines and creative confusions lie in wait for me.

And so I re-turn this circuit again and again; take a break, stretch my legs, remind myself why I write, what I write, and how it arrives, complete with whatever sensations the season offers. This time the lasting impression will be the flare of new leaves and the hoot of wild garlic.

Serious Noticing*
for Playful People

Put a notebook and pencil in your pocket when you go for a walk and pause somewhere interesting – or perhaps somewhere that doesn't look interesting but will turn out to be! – and try one or two of these brief activities. One act of attention captured into words seems to generate another and gradually we become more fluent.

1. **Tune up the senses**

   Get tuned into a place by denying your sense of sight. Spend five minutes with eyes closed paying attention to senses of sound, touch, smell, taste. Then write notes about the place with your eyes open. Hopefully you will have increased the other senses up to the 'volume' of sight.

2. **Look, but change the scale or viewpoint**

   If you were a mountaineer looking down on the place from that peak, or a bird soaring above, what would you see?

   Look closely at a feature – rock, lichen, moss, human skin, pavement – through a magnifying glass and imagine it is a vast plain or forest or city. Describe the experience of being within it.

---

* With thanks to James Wood for the term 'serious noticing'.

Look at it through a frame or upside down. What changes?

3. Examine Colour

Find some objects which match these paint colour names: velvet truffle; Nigerian sands; minted glory; Martian skies. Now find four coloured objects and give each a 'paint chart' name.

4. Give your environment life

Attribute actions (and carefully chosen verbs) to features that might appear passive. For example, if a river can carve, chew, smooth or tickle rocks, why can't a mountain or a building leer or loom or peer or preside?

List the essential qualities of a landscape feature, such as the uprightness, stillness, purple brush, pale trunks, dormancy of a stand of winter birch. What do they remind you of or make you think of? Write this as a metaphor, e.g: The waiting army of birches on the northern slopes of the glen.

5. Collecting

Collect some things which have been thrown away or washed up by a river or the sea. Write a story for one or two which gives 'useless' things a meaning.

6. Give things a voice

Attribute words or dialogue to landscape features. Find a tree or a building or a small plant considered a weed, things without any voice that we humans can recognise, and let it speak. It might get into a dialogue with another thing, or just talk. What does the willow tree say to you or to the river it leans over? You could ask it to pass on its wisdom to you.

7. Haiku

Collect two observations which relate to each other in an interesting way to create a bigger picture. Write them as a haiku (three lines of 5:7:5 syllables), experimenting with the words that express most succinctly what you mean. A haiku focuses on the natural world and highlights in short verse a brief moment in time, through vivid images. Typically, it conveys a sense of sudden enlightenment and can be read 'in one breath'.

8. Draw a map

You don't need to have great drawing skills to sketch the route and environment you passed through. Let myth play a part. Was there a threshold to pass through or a test of some sort? Use your own language and way of seeing things to create place-names. They might reflect physical characteristics of a place, e.g. 'Peak of the yew tree' or incidents that happened there, e.g. 'the hill of evil counsel' or even something it reminds you of, e.g. 'Mini Matterhorn', 'Pool of summer picnics'.

Acknowledgements

The essays listed below, or versions of them, have appeared in the following publications and sites:

A version of *Script and Scrape* was commissioned and published by Autumn Voices for 'Tales of Birnam and Dunkeld', 2022.

The Great Affair: Writing with the Flow was commissioned and released for audio by the Royal Literary Fund in 2021 as part of their 'Writers Aloud' series.

Lunar Cycling was commissioned and first published in 'Antlers of Water: Writing on The Nature and Environment of Scotland', edited by Kathleen Jamie. Canongate 2020/2021.

Getting away from it all? Royal Literary Fund 'Collected' series, 2017.

The Painting and the Verb, published in anthology Part 2 of 'All becomes Art' (Joan Eardley commemoration), Speculative Books 2022.

The Writer, The Island and the Inspiration, published in Northwords Now Issue 41, Spring–Summer 2021.

Where we are Least Alone, in 'Shelter Stone: The Artist and the Mountain', a public art project taking a limited-edition newsprint publication to 100 remote bothies, shelters and mountain huts across the UK, Iceland and the Alps, 2017/18.

How to be Free, Womankind magazine, 2018.

Acknowledgements

Weaving High Worlds, commissioned by the Cairngorms National Park Authority for 'Shared Stories: A year in the Cairngorms', editors Anna Fleming and Merryn Glover, 2019.

Joyous Messengers, commissioned by Open Book Reading for 'Unbound', 2021.

Street Play in Edinburgh, Walkhighlands magazine, 2016.

'Today I stand in a field and shout', Northwords Now 30, Autumn 2015. (http://www.corbenicpoetrypath.com/)

A Bubbling Immediacy, commissioned by Black & White Publishing as an introduction to a new paperback edition of 'The White Bird Passes' by Jessie Kesson, 2017.

The section of *Borrowed Boots* in italics is by Jenny Scanlan, first published in 'WORD PLAY: Original Work by the Penzance Ladies Book Club', 2006.

The Indoor Outdoor Writer, in 'The Bottle Imp', 2015.

Previous Publications

Life Drawing, Neil Wilson Publishing, 2000. Short story collection.

The Searching Glance, Salt Publishing, 2008. Short story collection.

A Wilder Vein, Two Ravens Press. Editor, anthology of non-fiction writing about the wild places of the British Isles, 2009.

Call of the Undertow, Freight Books, 2013. Novel.

Doubling Back: Ten paths trodden in memory, Freight Books, 2014. Narrative non-fiction.

The Other Side of Stone, Taproot Press, 2021. Fiction.

About the Author

Linda Cracknell is a writer of narrative non-fiction on the natural world, as well as of fiction and radio scripts. Her essay collection *Doubling Back: Ten Paths Trodden in Memory*, about journeys she took on foot in Scotland, Spain, Switzerland, and Kenya, was serialised on BBC Radio 4's *Book of the Week*, and she has won a Macallan/*Scotland on Sunday* literary prize as well as nominations for the Saltire Awards (Scotland's National Book Awards) and the Robin Jenkins Award for environmental writing. All of Linda's writing is inspired first and foremost by place, and she teaches nature and place writing and fiction writing.